START-UP SABOTEURS

Endorsements

"Start-ups are not for a weak stomach nor is this book. I have seen many start-ups launch without a true and honest self-assessment that would have saved them and others years of heartache, pain, and chaos. Ziad guides you through that assessment and jolts you with the start-up world's brutal realities to help protect you from the saboteurs—including yourself."

Katherine Malmay Bazemore
CEO and president, Cocoon Resources, Inc.,
a start-up venture firm

"*Start-Up Saboteurs* is a gutsy, uncompromising guidebook to creating true wealth and having the independence to say piss up a rope to those who wish to control your life. It dispenses true-to-life advice on establishing a winning mindset, building a strong team, pitching investors, facing down competition, and modifying your business to embrace disruption. Ziad's take no prisoner's book is to wealth creation what Richard Gatling's gun was to modern warfare. Stop wasting time; go and buy a copy. Now."

Stanford B. Silverman
Founder and CEO Minerva Capital Management,
a private equity group

"Ziad Abdelnour reminds me of a heavyweight fighter who comes after you relentlessly. He gets your attention right away. He makes you think and act differently. He doesn't pull any punches. As a veteran financier in private equity and the commodity markets, Ziad knows it's not easy for start-up to succeed, so he pushes you—hard—to reach your full entrepreneurial potential. He is the quintessential warrior and a one-of-a-kind leader born to win and create true wealth. If you follow the advice in Ziad's new book, you too will be a winner."

Mark Skousen
Investment expert and editor-in-chief
Forecasts & Strategies newsletter

Other Works

*Economic Warfare: Secrets of Wealth Creation
in the Age of Welfare Politics* (2011)

START-UP SABOTEURS

How INCOMPETENCE, EGO,
and SMALL THINKING
Prevent True Wealth Creation

ZIAD K. ABDELNOUR
Financier, Influencer, Author

NEW YORK

LONDON • NASHVILLE • MELBOURNE • VANCOUVER

START-UP SABOTEURS
How INCOMPETENCE, EGO, and SMALL THINKING PREVENT TRUE WEALTH CREATION

© 2020 **ZIAD K. ABDELNOUR**

Published in New York, New York, by Morgan James Publishing. Morgan James is a trademark of Morgan James, LLC. www.MorganJamesPublishing.com

ISBN 978-1-64279-695-7 paperback
ISBN 978-1-64279-696-4 eBook
Library of Congress Control Number: 2019908647

Cover Design by:
Rachel Lopez
www.r2cdesign.com

Interior Design by:
Bonnie Bushman
The Whole Caboodle Graphic Design

Morgan James is a proud partner of Habitat for Humanity Peninsula and Greater Williamsburg. Partners in building since 2006.

Get involved today! Visit
www.MorganJamesBuilds.com

This book is dedicated to the true serial entrepreneurs who live to the extreme. They push limits and spend their time building legacies. It is this legacy that ought to be transmitted to millions of entrepreneurs and financiers the world over.

True success is all about empowerment.

Geniuses are always marginalized to one degree or another. Someone wholly invested in the status quo is unlikely to disrupt it. Did you get to where you are by accepting the status quo? I didn't.

— Ziad K. Abdelnour

Contents

Foreword

By G. Chris Andersen

I have known Ziad Abdelnour for multiple decades. He's a no-nonsense decision-maker focused entirely on what makes business sense—just what a start-up entrepreneur needs in a top-notch advisor who has been there and done that successfully with skin in the game.

I remember years ago when Citibank retained Alvin Toffler (*Future Shock*) and me to help train their lending officers to recognize an entrepreneur. I got the impression they expected us to describe a gnome-like Swiss in Lederhosen and a funny hat with a boar's hairtail sticking out of it. It's not like that at all. I tried to get them to see that the way to recognize a real entrepreneur was to look over his shoulder and see if there wasn't a trail of transactions behind him.

Real entrepreneurs have tried and failed and gotten up and tried again. It's not an easy path but paying attention to some of the information in this book can truly help. This book is exceptional with live case studies to illustrate all. Ziad focuses entirely on getting rid of the myths and cutting out the BS. Basically, you must remember as an entrepreneur you are here to create wealth—that means create change—which is hard to do. I've said for years that you don't go to Wall Street to create income but to create wealth. It's even harder to do that as an entrepreneur than it is on Wall Street.

Unless you have personal wealth, the aspect of finding start-up capital is the first major obstacle which Ziad highlights. Failures are frequently due to arrogance and lack of experience. The entrepreneur better park that at the door. Ziad tells how to do it—and most importantly how to avoid it—by recognizing the needs of the potential financing sources.

Beating the start-up odds is also full of lessons worth paying attention to. Leave your feelings out of it and put the company's interests first, second, and third if you expect to succeed. Many entrepreneurs come up with an idea they pursue out of enthusiasm and passion. They don't understand that you don't find products for your customer; you need to find customers for your products.

With the benefit of hindsight, I see where I have failed that last one on many occasions. Failure is not the ultimate problem; that's one of the ways you learn. For many years I've been on the Junior Achievement of New York board, where we try to teach students how to build a business and become an entrepreneur. I am taken by Junior Achievement's history. One study showed that anyone who had gone through the organization's company's program was four times as likely to start a business in the first ten years after they got out of school. More telling to me was that anyone from JA who had started a first business had on average started four or five businesses. Obviously, some of those asked had failed, but they had learned from them and not been deterred.

My JA company got its capital from family. It came too easily. Then I had to create a product. Panic. Created a simple, stupid product.

After selling one to each of my investors, I was broke, bankrupt, and embarrassed. So I created a second company and sold my labor to another JA company that had too much business. Perhaps I invented outsourcing, and I paid off my investors plus a profit. Within a year I started my next company in an outsourcing of labor area.

How do you do that? First, face unpleasant truths early and forcefully. As a start-up entrepreneur you cannot afford to waste capital, whether financial or human, and you certainly cannot afford to waste time. Facing unpleasant realities helps you embrace the pain and move on to the next issue, which you will also have to overcome. There is a place for passion, but it should be to follow successes, not to ignore problems.

Sometimes the truths Ziad points out seem in conflict, like seeking advice from others but also bootstrapping for as long as possible so you can pursue your own plan and not answer to investors. Here again is that need for passion but balanced with the entrepreneur drive.

Ziad is particularly harsh about the role of venture capitalists. Venture capital is hard to get, hard to hold, and if you do get it, they start to take control of your financial future. Yes, they have more experience than you, and they are also the smartest guys in the room. But by and large they are not great finance guys. They only know one form of leverage (ha-ha): financing with their money, diluting your common equity. They also tend to take over control of financing, which means they want relatively quick high rates of return, which are generally the exact opposite of the entrepreneurs' vision for the ultimate future of the enterprise.

Ziad's sections on real-life expectations and the types of negotiation skills is especially relevant even if hard to implement. Never let them see you sweat. Remember; four out of five fail to raise their capital. Make sure that you stay around long enough to be the fifth. Try again.

Some of the things pointed out in this book may seem simplistic or obvious. Let one assure you that you'd be amazed that the number of times I've seen really smart people with great presentations blow a high probability opportunity just because of such simple errors and omissions. For instance, 90-plus percent of the people who come into my office have thought endlessly about what they want me to do for them but have not given any thought about what they should have been doing for me to make it easy to get a yes.

One thing you must take away from all of this is that it's imperative to be a salesman. You are always selling—for capital, for space, for the best help, for a better price point—but most of all you must sell yourself. Ziad does it brilliantly. He always has an end game in mind that shows how all parties win. Keep playing until you win. Then you're a true entrepreneur.

G. Chris Andersen
Founding partner
G.C. Andersen Partners LLC

Preface

Make no mistake about it; money is first and foremost about freedom. It is not about acquiring things nor flaunting it in front of family and friends. It is all about freedom. Freedom to do whatever you want, whenever you want. Freedom to tell your boss or whoever is running your life to take a hike. The only boss I want to have in my life is money. All the rest is for the birds. This is the key reason I immigrated to the United States back in 1982. To find freedom and make it big time. This is the reason I created Blackhawk Partners back in 2008.

Success is no accident or serendipity. I had all the odds against me, and I crushed each and everyone along the way. Not because I was a Democrat or a Republican. Not because of my attitudes about social issues. Not because of what my background is or isn't. Not because people think I'm a nice guy. I succeeded because I'm a capitalist, I'm an entrepreneur, and I'm a warrior. That is the mindset I want to teach others so they can create their own wealth and American success story.

I'm not here to entertain. This book is not going to be for everyone in the venture capital and entrepreneurial world, and that's okay. If you try to please everybody and worry about offending anybody, nothing is going to happen. You might make some money, but you certainly won't create wealth.

I'm an action-driven individual; too many people—including economists and academics in their ivory tower—watch from the sidelines and pontificate. *You should do this. You should do that.* But most of them have no skin in the game. They have nothing at risk, so they can talk the talk from now to the next century, and it's not going to make a difference.

A while back a guy came up to me and said: *I love what you write*, referring to all the blogs and articles I publish. Then he asked: *How do you make a living?* He expected me to answer: *Oh, I do this. I do that. I work here. I work there.* Instead I told him the reality: *I am not here to make a living.* He didn't expect that. But the truth is I don't work here and there. I don't make a living; I create wealth using the strategies, knowledge, and truths presented in this book.

I'm not an idealist. I'm a capitalist who wants to empower others to do what I did—find freedom. My uncle was a very successful guy—worked very hard, never got married—who lived to be ninety-one years old. Before he passed away I asked him: *How do you define success? Is it money? Is it power is it?* He told me it was none of the above. Success is about empowering people. The more you empower people, the more you are going to succeed.

I want to create a movement of smart, educated, well-informed, independent people and wrote this book to empower them to create their own wealth. And the best way to do that is by explaining how the system really works. *Start-up Saboteurs* is a guide to help striving entrepreneurs navigate through the challenging maze of egos, incompetence, and ignorance so they can separate fact from fiction. I cover it all. But in the end it comes down to this: To create real wealth you must abandon your limited thinking, eliminate boundaries, and stop defining the outcome. Most importantly it means not letting people motivated by jealousy, greed, and envy dictate what your limitations are.

You have to take risks in life. Your actions are what count.

Acknowledgments

This book could not have been written without first and foremost the support of my amazing family; Nada, Karl and Mark and my friend Kathleen Tracy, a writer of many talents whom I mentored at an accelerated rate on the fundamental workings of the financial world. In the process, she had to read every blog post I ever made, every magazine and video interview I've ever given, and everything I've ever published.

I am tremendously grateful to her and hope this will be a long partnership together, empowering more wealth creators, activists, and entrepreneurs worldwide by utilizing the synergy of our combined talents.

I am also grateful to Raoul Davis, my publicist and a man of many talents, a great friend and my key to the esteemed publishing house of Morgan James. This led me to David Hancock and his great team who were instrumental in publishing and promoting this work to the world. I am equally grateful to my son Mark Abdelnour who was the first one to review the first draft of my book and gave me invaluable insight into my manuscript. So proud of him. I guess as they say, every generation must outdo the previous one. This is what I call success and a full life.

I can honestly say I have been very blessed throughout my life with an amazing group of friends, influencers, and supporters—world citizens—who have provided me with insight and expertise second to none in the process of building my *business war machine*. They have influenced me, they have shaped me, they have humbled me, and they have made me a much better person.

I acknowledge the contributing influences of my larger-than-life role models, especially financiers Michael Milken, Marc Rowan, and Morty Davis; world-renowned academics, thinkers, and philosophers F. A. Hayek, Milton Friedman, and Arthur Brooks; the common sense, wisdom, and inspiration of the great political figures John F. Kennedy, Ronald Reagan, Donald J. Trump, and many more who have reinforced the notion of the American dream.

Although it would not be humanly possible to mention all, I would also like to particularly thank my inner circle of friends including but not limited to Katherine Malmay Bazemore, Stan Silverman, Tal Tsfany, and too many to enumerate in here—amazing individuals whose invaluable insights and feedback not only inspired me but thankfully held me to very high standards of quality while producing this great manuscript.

I must not forget my partners, board members, and other friends and supporters associated with the different organizations I have been instrumental in forming or in which I have held a leadership position over the past two decades. These include:

- Blackhawk Partners, Inc. http://blackhawkpartners.com and
- Financial Policy Council, www.financialpolicycouncil.org

I will also not forget all of the institutions, think tanks, and organizations which over the years provided me with an opportunity to share my thoughts with their constituents and debate the issues. These include:

- Freedom Fest, Las Vegas https://www.freedomfest.com
- Financial Times Conferences https://live.ft.com and
- Ayn Rand Institute https://ari.aynrand.org

They say a man is as good as the brain trust around him. I can humbly say I have assembled, over the years, one of the smartest and most empowering brain trusts around. It goes beyond borders and encompasses all ethnicities and religions. These exceptional men and women have one thing in common: a genuine pursuit of excellence and a sense of mission second to none. Finally, I wish to acknowledge the writers listed in the bibliography whose work provided resources for this book:

Thank you all for making this journey an adventure.

— **Ziad K. Abdelnour**

Introduction

It's All about
Wealth Creation, Stupid

Money is a form of wealth. But wealth is not necessarily money. Wealth encompasses much more than material possessions or cash; it includes resources. This book is all about wealth creation. This has been my theme, my philosophy for years. It's all about wealth creation.

It's about helping entrepreneurs develop a value proposition that explains what benefit the product or service provides, who they provide it for, and what will ultimately give their start-up an edge over the competition.

It is all about an Ayn Rand-esque philosophy embracing individualism and self-reliance. The government does not have a lot of answers, so the more we rely on the government, the more dependent we become, and the more we put our faith into the hands of others. I like the Chinese proverb that says you can give someone a fish or you can teach him how to fish. Enough of taking fish, it's time to teach people how to fish, how to create their own wealth. This is my mantra.

I want to create an army of people who think like this. There is nothing more impactful than changing people's lives by inspiring them and helping them create wealth, not for the sake of wealth, but for the sake of becoming free and independent. Nothing and no one will make you free and independent until you create your own fortress and fiefdom—wealth creation. That's the key.

What's happening in America today is you have a financial swamp that nobody is talking about. You have these elite venture capital firms in Silicon Valley and New York that just sit on pots of money. These venture capitalists have invested in a lot of failures. When you hear about Microsoft, Facebook, Apple—that's a very small number of success stories. Ninety-plus percent of VC investments have tanked. That money is clearly not being used to its best potential, a topic I will discuss at length in Part III.

Then, on the other hand, you have the entrepreneurs. A lot of them think they're gods, think they are the next Bill Gates. But they don't know how to get funded. So there's a huge disconnect here between those who have the money and the entrepreneurs who are seeking the money.

It's all about ego on both sides. This book is to basically bridge the gap and explain what gets funded, who should get funded, and why you get funded—basically the whole history and ecosystem of the VC world and of the entrepreneurial world in order to make a difference. It's about empowerment, and it's about education for entrepreneurs.

This book is brutally honest about what it really takes to build companies. I have financed more than 125 companies in my career, so I know what it takes, and I know what most are doing wrong. Almost all entrepreneurs make the same mistakes because of what they're taught at whatever elite business school they attend. With all due respect, most business schools spout theory because they aren't in the real-world trenches; they pontificate, they don't participate. A professor just gives you a theory: *Oh, you should expect to lose money in the first two or three years. It's normal because it's a start-up.* No, you don't have to, but it sinks into the students' minds. *This must be true because it's what I was taught.* I'm here to tell you what they taught you is wrong.

If somebody comes to me and says: *Ziad, this is my business plan. I need five million dollars and will start making money in year three.* I tell them to think about it differently. *If you had access to all the money in the world, what would it take you to make money six months after I fund you?* Ninety-nine percent of people respond that my scenario is impossible.

You're telling me that if I give you $100 million, you could not make money in six months? They aren't thinking like a businessman. They are thinking like a technologist and forget that they are here to make money—because it's not their money. If I had the choice between funding somebody who went to Harvard Business School then became a C-level executive at IBM versus a college dropout who went bankrupt three times with their start-ups, I would always fund the one who failed three times because he has likely learned from his mistakes. You only learn from your mistakes, from your failures, not from your successes.

I would also prefer them because they are likely to be much hungrier and eager to succeed; this is their passion. Many executives feel entitlement. *Because I graduated from here and worked there, I deserve to get whatever (money, perks, promotion, etc.) I ask for.* It's an attitude thing. Yes, the executive might have a track record but the guy who failed all those times wants to prove to the world that he can make it, which is why he's still in the race.

Many VCs choose to back people based on their names or their pedigrees, not what they have in their gut. It's all about style, optics, and appearances—not substance. The VCs are attracted to style and so are many entrepreneurs. Very few talk about substance. About track record. About skin in the game. About suffering, about guts, about courage. In many ways these values have become eroded during the last few generations and some may even say that they may have been lost for good. You learn to conform by having to follow what your parents say. When you go to school, you have to conform to what the teachers or principals say. You get a job and you have to conform to what your boss says. Society wants us to play nice. But innovation and forward thinking and leadership and wealth creation require individualism that often—inadvertently or not—steps on toes.

The best entrepreneurs buck conformity. Look at the so-called robber barons of the Industrial Age that built the United States into a super economic power. These captains of industry created the railroads, the steel industry, the auto industry, the tobacco industry, the oil industry, and banking as we know it today. Morgan, Rockefeller, Ford, Carnegie—these were killers. They were free-thinking entrepreneurs who found success through product innovation and business efficiency, and their affordable goods and services greatly improved the American standard of living.

Yes, there was another side of such wealth accumulation that made people uncomfortable: many of those industrialists used ruthless and unscrupulous—but not illegal—business practices on their way to then-unimaginable wealth, so they were depicted in popular culture and the media as having "robbed" the public. That is always the balancing act: finding the right set of checks and balances that both protect the public and workers but don't stifle innovation. For example, John D. Rockefeller's business practices growing Standard Oil was the inspiration for antitrust legislation known as the Sherman Antitrust Act, which was intended to protect the public and the economy by preventing a number of key industries being controlled by a limited number of individuals.

In 1911 the US Supreme Court ordered Standard Oil Trust to divest into thirty-three companies, which would function independently from each other. Ironically, the ruling ended up making Rockefeller America's first billionaire and one of the richest men in the world. Because he was a major stockholder, his net worth grew exponentially with the dissolution and establishment of new business entities. And he would go on to become one of the great philanthropists, giving hundreds of millions to colleges and toward medical research. And Rockefeller was also known as a fair employer who always paid good wages.

Usually it's not the wealth that people truly worry about. They might envy it, but they don't fear it. What they fear is an accumulation of power in too few hands—a cabal—because that can skew innovation, a subject we'll discuss in Part III.

Today's captains of industry are the likes of Bill Gates, Jeff Bezos, Larry Page and Sergey Brin, and the late Steve Jobs. We need more people like this. More individuals who don't conform to traditional or polite thinking. My mandate is to empower more people to become bigger-than-life killers who create wealth, not just money—but who do so without resorting to corruption, cheating, or exploitation of others.

Today we tend to focus on the unemployment rate being low. But just creating jobs isn't the point. Many of the jobs people have today don't even pay a living wage. Our focus needs to be on creating wealth, not just jobs or earning a wage.

Entrepreneurs are the backbone of America. They need the right education to know what's going on. They need to learn how to start thinking differently. They need to understand how to deal with the venture capitalists. They need to learn what it really takes to succeed. And that is what this book imparts, one step at a time. I don't provide broad brushstrokes; each chapter addresses a specific lesson, a specific reality that taken together will empower you and start you on the path toward both making money and creating wealth.

PART I

NOT ALL START-UPS
ARE CREATED EQUAL

Just as no two entrepreneurs are alike, there is no one-size-fits-all start-up. Your success in large part depends on knowing exactly what kind of company will best bring your vision to sustainable fruition. This section provides strategies for building the appropriate foundation for your start-up starting on day one.

Chapter 1

The History of
American Start-Ups

Trust your instincts, know what you want, and believe in your ability to achieve it. Rules and conventions are important for schools, businesses, and society in general, but you should never follow them blindly.

— **Biz Stone**

The conviction that we live in the land of opportunity for entrepreneurs is part of the American DNA. Throughout United States history anybody with a good enough idea, strong enough determination, and a committed willingness to work hard believed they could successfully start a business and prosper. It could be easily argued that this country was built by bootstrapping self-starters, although the goals of those entrepreneurs have changed over the centuries as have their start-ups.

According to Steve Blank at the *Wall Street Journal*, there are six types of start-ups today: lifestyle, small business, scalable, buyable, social, and inside a large company. That's because not all entrepreneurs want the same thing, and not all start-ups are designed for the same purpose. The differences are of intent, scale, and aspiration.

Buyable start-ups mostly refer to mobile app start-ups that are created for the express purpose of getting acquired by a bigger company. Technology has advanced to the point where the cost required to build a product is relatively minimal. Combine that with how quickly these products can come to market, the insatiable appetite for phone apps, and an abundance of angel capital willing to invest $100,000 to $1 million—a pittance in tech start-up terms—has attracted a steady stream of entrepreneurs looking to build and flip start-ups for usually six-figures. They make money to create their next app, and investors get a return. Win-win.

Sometimes large, established companies develop a **start-up in-house** in an effort to launch new products to keep the company relevant to consumers or take advantage of new technology or new cultural trends. Sometimes the start-up is for an innovating new product, but usually it's just a variation of core products because large, established companies have a harder time developing truly innovative products outside their envelope.

Social start-ups refer to businesses founded to basically make the world a better place, not to make the entrepreneur rich, at least not in a material sense. This kind of start-up has been around throughout modern times and hasn't changed much over the centuries.

The flipside of the socially conscious do-gooder is the **lifestyle start-up** entrepreneurs. Consider the person who starts a ski lesson business. They attract enough business to pay the bills so they can spend the rest of their time on the slopes. California beaches are full of dive shops and surfing rental stores run by entrepreneurs who earn a comfortable enough living so they can continue to pursue their personal passions of surfing or diving. These are lifestyle entrepreneurs who have no greater aspirations than living the life they love.

The vast majority of American entrepreneurs run **small business start-ups.** Small businesses make up more than 99 percent of all companies and employ half of all non-governmental workers. Small businesses include probably the places you visit the most: hairdressers, mechanics, plumbers, electricians, your favorite local restaurant, the dry cleaners—these entrepreneurs are anyone who runs their own business.

This type of entrepreneur might be the hardest working. They serve the local community and either hire locally or employ family. Most are profitable—but often just barely. A small business is more than a description; it is a mindset. Small businesses are not designed for scale; these entrepreneurs simply want to own their own business and take care of their family. Their finances are basic. If they need additional capital, it comes from their own savings, from relatives, or a small business loan from their local bank. Small business entrepreneurs might not be built to grow into million-dollar enterprises, but they are by far the backbone of entrepreneurship and local economies.

This category of entrepreneur has been around since colonial days when they opened small local businesses as blacksmiths, publishers, carpenters, lumberers, gunsmiths, silversmiths, milliners, breweries, candlemakers, tavern owners, and innkeepers. Back then all businesses were small because of logistical, economic, and technological limitations. Communication was limited and transportation confined to local communities before the onslaught of national railroads. Nor were there any banks. In many cases commodity money—animal skins, wampum, and tobacco—served as the method used for buying and selling as paper money and coins were scarce. But beyond that, small businesses were trusted. Early Americans retained a distrust of large companies and big government, seeing them as a threat to personal liberty. According to historian James L. Houston wrote in the *American Historical Review*: "Americans believed that if property was concentrated in the hands of a few … those few would use their wealth to control other citizens, seize political power, and warp the republic into an oligopoly."

Thomas Jefferson believed small businesses were the very cornerstone of the would-be new country, saying, "The end of democracy and the defeat of the American Revolution will occur when government falls into the hands of lending institutions and moneyed corporations."

The Boston Tea Party happened because local merchants and tradesmen were worried that the East India Company, then the world's largest corporation, was selling low-priced tea in the colonies, and had that continued it would have driven local business to ruin. (Two centuries later, Walmart's low-prices did in fact ruin many small businesses in most of the areas where the company opened a store, so the colonists weren't just being paranoid.)

Even after gaining independence from Britain, the concern over powerful companies that hoarded wealth prompted the new federal government to institute severe restrictions on the creation of corporations, and the freshly-minted state governments followed suit, restricting a corporation's size, profitability, geographic reach, and even how long they could exist. That is not to say small businesses have never broken the mold and jumped categories. Some of the United States' most venerable companies that still exist began during that time as small businesses including Jim Beam distillery, Bowne stationers, Ames, the country's first shovel company, Bakers chocolate, and Caswell-Massey soaps.

Whereas the small business designation is one informed by limits of size, vision, and scale, **scalable start-ups**—what most people think of when they hear the term *start-up*—are identified by the ambition to grow-fast and conquer wide. Today they are probably most closely associated with Silicon Valley tech companies, but start-ups as we think of them today go back more than one hundred years. For example, in 1909 Dr. Leo Baekeland—called the father of the plastic industry—patented Bakelite, the world's first synthetic plastic. Three years later he formed the General Bakelite Company to manufacture and market his new engineered material that would be used in a range of electronic products such as phones, radios, and stereos. The company merged with two others in 1926 and Baekeland would die a very wealthy fellow.

While working at the Buffalo Forge Company, Willis Carrier patented the first electrical air conditioning unit in 1906. When his employer passed on producing his innovation, Carrier and six other young engineers pooled their life savings of $32,600 and started Carrier Engineering Corporation to manufacture and distribute heating, ventilation, and air conditioning (HVAC) systems. Up until then, air conditioning was the domain of the super-wealthy. Carrier wanted to bring comfort to the masses and took advantage of a huge market. As of 2012, it was a $12.5 billion company with more than 43,000 employees serving customers in 170 countries on six continents.

One of Silicon Valley's first success stories is now hi-tech lore. In 1939 Bill Hewlett and Dave Packard launched HP out of a garage in Palo Alto. Their first product was a precision audio oscillator, which they sold to Walt Disney among others. But their road to legend was with high-quality electronic test and measurement equipment. The company is credited with creating the first personal computer, the first handheld scientific electric calculator, and introduced both inkjet and laser printers for the desktop. HP's innovations served as a springboard for other companies.

Another famous story is how Steve Wozniak originally designed the Apple I computer while working at HP and offered it to Packard and Hewitt because they had the right of first refusal for employees' creations. But they passed because they wanted their company to stay focused on the scientific, business, and industrial markets. So Wozniak ended up starting Apple with Steve Jobs. The power of empowerment; the freedom of choice.

The key to most start-up successes is seeing a need and filling it. In 1962 Sam Walton's business model was to target areas neglected by retail stores, and by 2018 there were a total of 5,358 Walmart stores throughout the United States with net sales of more than $14 billion. Similarly, in 1971 Herb Kelleher thought the time was right for a discount airline to make flying more affordable for the average traveler and founded Southwest Airlines, which serviced neglected areas and provided a low-cost, no-frills option, along with a company culture of self-deprecating humor. Consumers responded, and Southwest is now one of the largest airlines in the United States and has enjoyed more than forty straight years of profitability.

The list goes on and on, from well-known iconic companies like Microsoft, Google, and Facebook to relative unknowns like Acuity Surgical, GYMGUYZ, and Defense Logistics that have gone from start-up to multi-million and billion-dollar businesses. What all these companies have in common is that they were scalable start-ups, which is what venture capital investors crave to bankroll. And what scalable start-up entrepreneurs aspire to build. They never thought small; they had a vision they believed could change the world, or at least their corner of it.

Unlike small business entrepreneurs, these founders were not concerned with earning a long-term living; from the start their eyes were on the prize of creating equity in a company that would eventually go public, providing them with a multigenerational wealth level payoff. You shouldn't be surprised that these types of start-ups are the least common, mostly because they are the hardest to realize.

They are also the riskiest because of the steep capital these start-ups often want—whether they require it is another issue. So enter the venture capitalists. Technically, their job is to seek out start-ups that have a repeatable and scalable business model, then finance it for fast-growth. Sounds simple enough. But it hasn't worked out that way; why is debatable.

The Rise of the Lean Start-Up

Some of today's younger entrepreneurs won't remember the dotcom crash of 2000, the dramatic end of a five-year-long dotcom bubble that started with the Netscape IPO in 1995. Suddenly Internet tech start-ups were proliferating like an aggressive black mold. And VCs were climbing over one another to get in on the action and public offerings were providing risk capital at scale. The problem was the IPOs, and subsequent stock prices had no bearing in reality on actual revenue and profits. It was fueled mostly by irrational expectations.

Start-up founders wrote business plans filled with exuberant forecasts without a thought to product-market fit. But it didn't matter because the assumption was they'd raise more money when needed through an IPO. The actual process of creating a business plan, raising money, then executing the plan wasn't the issue as much as the sheer volume of start-ups flooding the market. It was unsustainable, and inevitably IPO money shriveled.

After the dotcom bubble burst, angel investment dried up, and most corporate VCs closed. The remaining VC money was scarce and mostly out of reach, meaning start-up funding was essentially nowhere to be found.

Enter the lean start-up model. Proponents argued that too often VCs—as well as academics—had approached start-ups as if they were just a mini-me version of established large companies that work under established business models. Lean start-up advocates state that start-ups by nature have to search for a scalable and repeatable business model because you can't judge a market beforehand.

Traditionally, entrepreneurs developed a multiyear business plan first then used that plan to raise money so they could develop the product and establish the start-up. The lean start-up process calls for entrepreneurs to search for a business by testing their ideas, by building a prototype or releasing some other trial balloon, then using customers feedback to determine their next direction. The main point is that it's driven by a *fail fast, fail cheap* mentality.

The whole lean start-up process was designed to minimize the time and money invested in start-ups by developing products that consumers are known to want within an existing market, rather than coming up with a new product or service that requires cultivating customer demand and having to create a market from scratch,

To me the lean start-up is a solution to the problem created by trying to do everything as tech start-ups in Silicon Valley. The primary reason lean start-ups had to hunt for markets was that they were in the wrong geographical place.

At some point you should get out of the building—or in this case, California—to be an entrepreneur. A start-up focusing on making money by delivering mobile banking services in Africa should be located … in Africa. Anywhere else is idiotic. Ninety percent of the opportunities require you to leave the building, and better geographical distribution of entrepreneurial talent and money is merely one way to make the capital markets smarter.

Looking Forward

First-time and aspiring entrepreneurs often mistakenly believe that a completely unique and original idea is what's going to make them rich. In reality success has very little to do with the idea and more about the team, execution, persistence, timing, and how good one is at adapting the business along the way. For example, pick the right market, and it will help cover most sins of execution.

It is time to stop making the same stupid mistakes that are holding you and your start-up back and preventing you from heading down the path to true wealth.

More than half of all start-ups fail within the first five years; two-thirds by year ten. In the next chapter I'll explain the steps you must take—and not take—to beat those odds.

Chapter 2

Beating the Start-Up Odds

Once you embrace unpleasant news not as a negative, but as evidence of a need for change, you aren't defeated by it.
— **Bill Gates**

Being an entrepreneur is not for the faint of heart. Before you raise your first dollar in capital or make your first sales call, the odds are already against you. According to the US Bureau for Labor Statistics, 50 percent of all new business fail by their fifth year, and only one-third make it to the tenth year.

I am not surprised. Each year I listen to more than five hundred pitches from entrepreneur hopefuls. Some have experience; some don't. Out of the hundreds of founders that enter my office, only about ten walk away with a deal. I am always taken aback by the number of people who come in and are clearly not ready to take on the business world, whether out of ignorance, ego, or a simple lack of preparedness. Rather than a how-to, I want to give you a how-not-to, a primer on avoiding stupid mistakes and giving your start-up a fighting chance.

Ego Adsum

Start-ups fail for a lot of different reasons, but one I see repeatedly is ego. It presents as a dangerous sense of self-importance. Or the entrepreneur thinks they are the smartest person in the room who knows better than anyone else and either doesn't seek out advice or doesn't want to listen when it's offered. Such know-it-alls delude themselves into thinking they have everything figured out, even though they don't. For as hard as it is to elbow your way into the marketplace in ideal circumstances, it's made exponentially harder when you don't check your ego at the door.

The famous psychoanalyst Carl Jung recognized the dangers of a bloated ego and warned: "An inflated consciousness is always egocentric and conscious of nothing but its own existence. It is incapable of learning from the past, incapable of understanding contemporary events, and incapable of drawing the right conclusions about the future. It is hypnotized by itself and therefore cannot be argued with. It inevitably dooms itself to calamities that must strike it dead."

In other words, little good comes from an outsized sense of self.

It's been joked that ego is an invisible line item on every start-up's profit and loss statement. But it's no laughing matter when an entrepreneur puts their own priorities and self-esteem before the needs of their start-up. One study found that more than a third of respondents admitted that all of their failed business decisions were driven by ego. Don't wait for hindsight to see 20-20 that ego needs to be controlled and channeled so it can work for the good of the start-up.

By definition and in practice, ego is not an inherently bad thing. We all have an ego. It's what drives our confidence, gives us optimism, and fuels ambition. It allows us to accept challenges, overcome doubt and fear. Without ego we would never accomplish anything of note. When ego is kept in perspective and used to complement our skill-sets, our knowledge, and our goals, it can be a powerful, positive force.

The problems arise when you let your egos dominate your actions, when your sense of importance starts having no basis in reality. That's when confidence turns to arrogance, self-assurance becomes self-centeredness, optimism digresses into conceit. When egos overinflate and get in the way, it's difficult if not impossible to make good decisions that will positively impact your business.

In some cases egos overinflate after achieving some success. *Look at what I did. Aren't I great?* It gets pumped up by the person's mistaken belief, by the illusion, that they alone were responsible for the achievement. Ego also convinces them any future project or efforts will automatically be just as, if not more, successful. Sometimes it works out that way although not very often. But in my experience too often entrepreneurs' egos are unrealistically burnished by VCs. They are blind to their mistakes because they're being brainwashed by VCs telling them how brilliant they are before they even open for business—a self-serving strategy. Competition between VCs is intense, so the goal is to snatch up a promising team and business plan before the VC next door. Making the budding entrepreneur feel good about themselves is just part of the game.

Behavioral economics tells us that humans are short-sighted by nature. We are wired to seek evidence confirming what we already believe and to ignore evidence that contradicts it. We are usually overconfident, underestimating how much we don't know. That leads to tunnel vision, bad decisions, and myopic judgments that can lead your start-up to fail.

The irony is that failure and the ego-driven mistakes that helped undermine your business also tend to widen your range of experience and shrink your ego. Few things are as humbling as your business crashing and burning. We seek confirmatory evidence, or external affirmation, of our own decisions because it allows us to avoid the mental exertion of change. The ego is always for the status quo because in the status quo you are alive; there's no risk to your life and carefully maintained identity.

So you can improve your odds of success by not becoming a slave to your ego. It's a little bit like fire; when controlled it gives us warmth, safety from predators, and food. When it's uncontrolled, it incinerates us. As with all things, balance is critical, so an important tool for any entrepreneur is ego-management, which is based on humility, curiosity, and a thirst for truth.

Humility is the flipside of pride. It doesn't mean suddenly being selfless; it means realizing that others might have a better answer than you or a better solution. It means accepting you might not always be the smartest person in the room. Being confident and humble are not mutually exclusive. Embracing humility will help give you an open mind and a clearer vision of how to beat the odds and make your start-up a success.

Once you have a more open mind, your curiosity will be freer so you will be more apt to first ask questions rather than just barking out answers that may not be the best way forward. The best entrepreneurs are the most curious, and many of the greatest innovations are all born from that curiosity. The default state is to try and avoid a blow to our manufactured identity. People will often avoid asking questions or consider other views because they fear how they'll appear should it contradict something they've previously stated so confidently.

Lastly, without seeking truth it is unlikely you will find success. The truth very well might set you free, but it's not always fun. People say they want the truth, but more accurately, they want the truth that is easy to hear. They don't want the painful truths that don't support our decisions or force us to accept we were wrong about something. But without truth, you will never be able to course-correct. Putting the company first and your bruised feelings second is an important step in saving your start-up from failure.

Don't Deny the Obvious

If you make a mistake, don't spend precious time and energy trying to deny it or point the finger at someone else. Be a leader and own it, then spend your time and energy fixing the problem. As I've already noted, start-ups often fail because founders want to be seen as the smartest person in the room, which means not being wrong. Making a mistake is going to happen. None of us is perfect. But the difference between success and failure is how you handle that mistake.

Acknowledging mistakes makes you accountable not only to yourself but to everyone else. And being accountable shows responsibility. If you have forgotten an important appointment, don't blame your assistant. Pick up the phone, call the person you were supposed to meet, apologize, and reschedule. Being honest can diffuse a lot of other people's annoyance in part because it's unexpected and refreshing. If you have misjudged inventory, meaning some product delivery is going to be late, don't point fingers at the shipping or transportation department or try to blame the weather. Immediately contact your customers, accept the responsibility, and work out a solution to minimize the problem. Not owning up to a mistake can create other fires that can quickly escalate and engulf you.

Many entrepreneurs resist to owing up to the conditions that created the shortcoming—conditions they themselves may have contributed to. They need to put ownership of the problem above the egotistical need of always wanting to look good. If they don't, failure will result.

Also, character counts, both yours and your start-up. If you want success and longevity for your business, earning a reputation for integrity is crucial. People want to work with people and companies they can trust. Trying to hide a mistake and hope nobody notices or passing the buck does not inspire confidence or respect—from anyone, employees, vendors, or customers alike. Owning up shows integrity and whatever embarrassment you may feel is worth it because in the end people will likely trust you more going forward. It's not the mistake that is a deal-breaker, it's being dishonest about it.

Don't Force a Square Peg into a Round Hole

It sounds so basic, but that's probably why it's so often overlooked by entrepreneurs. A big reason some start-ups fail is that they should never have been businesses to begin with. You don't need an air conditioning company in the Arctic or a liquor store in a dry Mississippi county. If there is no market for the product or service you want to sell, you're doomed to failure.

Take the short-lived company called Washboard. The company was based on the premise that people who live in apartments or condos without their own washer and dryer are always short of quarters come laundry day. So Washboard would send customers a roll of quarters (worth $20) that with shipping and handling fee would cost $27. That start-up quickly went out of business.

That was a case where there simply wasn't enough of a value proposition for consumers. If you have to go to the laundromat anyway, they have coin change machines. If you live in a condo, presumably you go to the grocery store where you can get quarters without a surcharge. There was no reasonable belief that enough people would be willing to pay a 35 percent convenience fee for a product (quarters) they can get a lot of other places for free.

While Washboard may be an extreme example of a company with no market, there are thousands of examples each year of start-ups that don't address and solve a real problem. There will always be new problems to solve because the world is always changing. Charles Holland Duell, who was the commissioner of the US Patent and Trademark Office in the early 1900s, once famously said, "Everything that can be invented has been invented." He was wrong then, and he'd be wrong now. The more complex the world becomes, the more problems there are to solve. But to beat the odds of start-up failure, the bigger the problem you solve, the better your chances. As the saying goes, sell the problem you solve, not the product.

That said, it still boils down to sales. You can have the most innovative idea in the world, but without a well thought out distribution strategy and a viable path to sales, you'll be just another one in the half of ventures that fail.

Timing Is Everything

Often an entrepreneur's idea is good, but the timing isn't. They could be late for a trend and found an overcrowded market or they are ahead of their time either as far as consumer behavior, vendor comfort level, or current infrastructure. Kozmo.com was a VC-funded start-up that offered free same-day delivery for videos, games, DVDs, food, and Starbucks coffee in several major cities in the United States. It was founded by two young investment bankers in March 1998 in New York City, and was out of business by April 2001, losing hundreds of millions in value in the dotcom crash.

The start-up failed because they didn't make money on their services. And they didn't make money on their services because at that time the infrastructure wasn't there. The founders believed the savings companies would achieve by not needing to rent space for retail stores would exceed the costs of delivery. But the idea of a virtual store, Amazon notwithstanding, was still new. Then, their refusal to charge a fee was the final nail in the coffin. Today, same-day delivery is part of many companies' offerings, but Kozmo's timing was a few years too early.

Don't Assume

Another reason so many start-ups fail is the flawed assumption that if the product is good enough, consumers will find it, the *Field of Dreams* philosophy of *Build it and they will come.* Except a lot of times, they don't. Founders can be overly optimistic when it comes to acquiring customers instead of better preparing for what is usually a time consuming and expensive aspect of growing a business.

It's not unusual for the cost of acquiring the customer to actually be higher than the value of that customer—not a path to sustainable success. The short-sightedness I often see when it comes to figuring out a realistic cost of customer acquisition is another main reason so many start-ups fail. Even before you look for capital, you need to figure out a scalable plan to acquire customers and then to monetize those customers at a high enough level to more than offset the cost of acquisition.

Once the business is up and running, you need to monitor that plan, realizing the ongoing cost to acquire customers or clients goes beyond ad placement or tv spots. You need to include the entire marketing ecosystem from lead generation to sales salaries/commission. These aspects of running a business aren't as glamorous or fun as appearing on panels or getting interviewed at trade shows, but they are integral to surviving five years and beyond.

Don't Think You Have to Be Perfect

You don't need to come up with a game-changing solution to every problem. If you develop tunnel-vision on each and every hiccup, you will inevitably lose sight of the big picture and not be able to sustain your business. Those who think more in terms of turning a negative outcome into a positive potential have a much better chance of riding out the rough times.

At the same time you can't just throw your hands up in surrender at the first crisis or when things take an unexpected turn, such as a late shipment, customer defections or lack of payment, or weather delays. If there is one constant, it's that markets are not always consistent. They are complex and difficult to accurately predict. As the case studies in Part III of this book show, businesses will be quick to fail if the founder lacks persistence, the skill to quickly adapt to changing circumstances, or the ability to see around corners and think ahead.

Sometimes a start-up can do everything right and still fail. I always say one of the hardest parts of life is deciding whether to walk away or try harder. But in the end you must be a realist as well as an optimist. Don't construe a failure as a permanent defeat. Accept it as a learning experience and a challenge. Take the time to understand what went wrong then use that assessment to improve your odds with your next start-up.

And for true entrepreneurs, there is always a next time.

Chapter 3

Harsh Truths Start-Up CEOs Must Face

Nothing is more creative—or destructive—than a brilliant mind with a purpose.

—Dan Brown

After thirty years in the business, here's my observation: most start-up founders are a bunch of inexperienced, arrogant people who for the most part are terrible at making money because they make fundamental mistakes. Blind to their shortcomings, they maintain irrationally high self-esteem—no wonder more than half will fail within five years. It's time for an attitude adjustment so you can focus on what's important, starting with being brutally honest with yourself.

Founders often highlight what looks good and hide what looks bad. You can't make an informed decision when in denial so fake traction must be avoided at all cost. This isn't a modern phenomenon; it's human nature. It's just more noticeable now that we live in a global economy with so much more money on the line and each failure broadcast via real-time communication around the world.

Starting a business isn't for the overly sensitive, the know-it-alls, or the paranoid, so I'm here to tell you some harsh truths, such as being creative and clever is no guarantee of success. I'm approached every year by hundreds of entrepreneurs who mistakenly believe that their unique or original idea is what's going to make them rich. They don't understand that a sustainable business has very little to do with the idea and more about the choice of market and value proposition.

I'm a devotee of Sequoia Capital's Don Valentine who preaches that if you pick the right market, it will help cover most sins of execution. He gives the example of how once his firm saw Apple's explosion, they started investing in other companies in that ecosystem and made incredible returns. But put a brilliant team in a bad market, and no amount of smarts or agility will overcome that handicap. There are countless brilliant and dedicated entrepreneurs who stupidly went after bad market segments, burning through hundreds of millions of VC money with little return to show for it. And no amount of pivoting could have saved those investments.

Similarly, business models and not just products should be considered. People tend to focus far too much on the product idea. But if you can't make the economics work, then no matter how great your product or service is, you'll end up in the dead pool. So do yourself a big favor and start spending more time thinking about business models and markets before getting funded.

What we're talking about here is execution. History is littered with forgotten inventors who had innovative ideas and strategies but poorly executed them. Those we remember took ideas that were floating around in the ether and actually made something happen. In my experience, just about every successful venture is based on an unoriginal idea that is beautifully executed. Show an investor you can execute on a solid idea, and you will not only get funded but be well-positioned to succeed.

Tempering Ego

Ego is a double-edged sword. On one hand it is vital. Webster's defines ego as self-esteem. Entrepreneurs need a healthy ego to succeed because you must believe in yourself and be confident in your ability to build a business. I have found that most successful people exhibited a very high level of self-esteem long before they achieved success. They knew in their hearts that they deserved success. The lack of sufficient self-esteem and self-confidence is what inhibits many entrepreneurs from fulfilling their quest to start a company. Winners in all fields are confident in their ability to achieve their ideals.

But too much of a good thing can be dangerous. Water is necessary for life but drinking too much in one sitting can literally kill you. Likewise, an inflated, pathological ego will get in the way of your objectivity, skew your perspective, and sabotage your efforts for success sooner or later.

Leadership expert Robin S. Sharma once noted: "Leadership is not a popularity contest; it's about leaving your ego at the door. The name of the game is to lead without a title." What he means is that you will not have all the answers. You must be willing to listen to others, to admit there might be a better path than the one you chose. You must be willing to share the credit because it's not just all about you; it should be about what's best for the company. You must be able to delegate because you're not the only one capable.

According to research by the Biotechnology and Biological Sciences Research Council people rely on their past experiences when making current decisions. That can often be beneficial. But when ego makes you reject new information and facts that diverge from your personal experience—such as when dealing with market changes or new technology—that can hinder your start-up's progress. You need to recognize when a problem can't be solved based on your old answers.

Part of the problem is that many entrepreneurs feel the pressure to have all the answers all the time. That is stupid. Nobody knows everything, especially today when markets and technologies can change so fast. So don't make the egotistical mistake of associating ignorance about a certain topic with weakness. It's only a weakness if you are unwilling to admit you need to learn. If you don't ask questions, you won't be able to adapt to changing business conditions and new circumstances. Pretending to know something about a unique situation is detrimental to you as a person and your company's future.

Bloated egos can also drive founders to make decisions designed to maintain their public image, even if it might not be in the long-term best interests of their start-up. They don't want to admit mistakes or acknowledge they need to pivot because for the oversized ego, failures tend to be overly personal. That perhaps is the most stupid attitude of all because learning by making mistakes is an inherent part of all innovation. Success only thrives in environments where people feel free to experiment, are open to exploring ideas, and can readily admit failure. As Bill Gates said, "Once you embrace unpleasant news not as a negative, but as evidence of a need for change, you aren't defeated by it."

Here's another truth entrepreneurs need to understand—today. Stop being so ridiculously secretive about your precious idea. So many entrepreneurs are terrified someone will steal their idea. This is one of the most stupid beginner blunders and shows a real lack of business sophistication. The odds of you coming up with a genuinely never-before-thought-of idea or concept is slim to none.

Ever heard of zeitgeist? It means *the spirit of the time*. It's the reason why you'll see three TV shows come on the same season about the same topic. Not because anyone stole the others' idea but because the times we live in direct our perceptions, prompt our ideas, and dictate our solutions to current problems. Nobody's coming up with a better blacksmith anvil because that has nothing to do with the times we live in. But everyone and their uncle in the auto industry is trying to come up with an affordable, stylish, practical electric car that goes five hundred miles or more per charge.

All the secrecy bullshit is just that, so get over yourself. Smart founders should, in fact, do the exact opposite and talk about their value-proposition to everyone out there to perfect their idea. And guess what? The people you are so fearful will steal your idea are too busy working on their own big ideas to worry about yours. So please stop wasting people's time by asking them to sign those ridiculous and invariably useless NDAs before discussing your start-up.

One of the more difficult truths most entrepreneurs struggle with is the need to delegate. Being a founder or CEO does not mean being hands-on with everything. While developing the idea for the start-up and getting it off the ground, entrepreneurs are often on their own, a one-man-band. They see the business as their offspring and are possessive and proprietary.

If you want your business to have any chance of growing, you have to let go, hire the smartest, most trustworthy people you can find or afford, and transition to a leadership role. Otherwise you will just get in the way of your company's potential success. The only things you should not delegate in the early stages of a business are fundamentals like customer engagements, raising capital, and ensuring product-market fit.

Another truth people have a hard time digesting is you are not helping yourself or your company by asking business advice from your best friend or your dear grandpa. That is a terrible mistake (unless they happen to be Oprah and Paul Mitchell respectively). Your friends love you. Anything you pitch will not be judged objectively. If you want a truly honest response, say the idea is from someone else they aren't connected with, and you'll get more objective feedback. But that's a band-aid.

Entrepreneurs—both young and established—too often listen to bad advice from the wrong people. With all the hype over entrepreneurship, the quantity of information has gone way up while the quality has gone way down, meaning unqualified sources are everywhere. The biggest danger is that when you finally do get good advice, if it conflicts with bad advice you were previously told, you might not recognize it for what it is.

Learning how to separate good advice from bad is a learned skill. But a good rule of thumb is to listen to professionals who have been at it much longer than you. Surround yourself with smart financiers and advisors you can trust. Pick their brains. Offer them stock in your new venture.

The thing about advice is that whether it's good or bad is often subjective; what's good for your company may be bad for someone else's. Smart entrepreneurs follow a hybrid of advice, created from suggestions from many professionals. That's why it is so important to have mentoring conversations with a variety of people. And it's okay to disagree with someone regardless of their credentials if their advice doesn't fit your circumstance. Sometimes understanding why their advice won't work ultimately clarifies the direction you should go. While it's fine to turn to family and friends for moral support, unless they are business owners or financiers with experience and a track record, leave advice to the professionals.

Finally, the truth that is hardest to hear: stop with the passion crap. I have seen too many founders so blinded by passion for their initial product or service that they were incapable of pivoting or changing even when the market is screaming at them to. The trick is to get passionate about product-market fit, not about the product as it is today. You must be willing to keep tweaking until you find the fit.

In an interview, Mark Cuban once observed that the worst advice he hears people give or get is: *Follow your passion.*

"What a bunch of BS. Why? Because everyone is passionate about something. Usually more than one thing. We are born with it. There are always going to be things we love to do, that we dream about doing, that we really, really want to do with our lives. Those passions aren't worth a nickel. If you really want to know where your destiny lies, look at where you apply your time. Time is the most valuable asset you don't own. You may or may not realize it, but how you use or don't use your time is going to be the best indication of where your future is going to take you."

In other words, take perseverance over inspiration every day. Don't follow your passion; follow your effort. That alone might not lead to results, but without it, you won't have results.

Now, not getting wrapped up in following *a* passion is not to say you shouldn't *have* passion. Creating wealth requires work. It requires drive. It requires sacrifice. And it most definitely requires a burning desire not only toward your businesses but toward everything in life as well. Passionate people sweat the details, they're curious, and they care. That's what really matters to building a larger-than-life business. An intense passion for creating success, wealth, legacy, or fame is the primary motivator for most top entrepreneurs. They set their goals high, and when those are attained, they set new ones even higher.

Lastly, any entrepreneurs dreaming of a fast flip to riches need the biggest attitude adjustment of all. Start-ups are a marathon, not a sprint. The average successful exit takes seven to ten years of hard work, sacrifice, eighty-hour workweeks, luck, and failure, pivoting, and then sustaining. If you don't have the commitment, patience, or passion, don't waste your time—and everyone else's—trying to find an even bigger moron to back your business. It will be a total exercise in futility. But if you invest the time to understand the market, build a motivated team, and learn to execute effectively, then the wealth will come.

Chapter 4
Business Capital 101

Money is always eager and ready to work for anyone who is ready to employ it.

— **Idowu Koyenikan**

In the film and TV series business, it's all about content. Without a script there is no movie or television episode or documentary. It all starts with a writer putting the story on paper. It's an industry that begins and ends with its storytellers, which is why you hear studio executives and television network presidents always say *content is king.*

In the start-up world, ideas may be the currency, but here capital is king. Whether you want to open a local food truck business, a nonprofit to maintain a local wetland, or have the most innovative solution to one of the world's biggest problems, if you don't have the money to develop that idea, it's nothing more than daydreaming.

I've sometimes heard entrepreneurs identify themselves as idea people, not businessmen. As if the work to secure money is somehow beneath them. How stupid. Time for a reality check. If you want that brilliant idea to become a reality, you better get off your creative high horse and put on your big-boy business pants. Being an entrepreneur isn't for the timid—or the ignorant.

You don't need an MBA from an elite Ivy League school to find funding and be successful, but you do need to understand the start-up ecosystem, which is an environment that can be comprised of mentors, investors, academia, incubators, associations, or government organizations that provides the entrepreneur access to great ideas, talent, funding, and customers. Coming up with a viable idea is often the easiest part; nurturing it to fruition is the challenge, and it starts with capital. Eighty percent of would-be start-ups fail to secure the money they need to get off the ground. That's a lot of potentially great products and services that have ended up in the cemetery.

Part of the problem is too many first-time entrepreneurs who try to enter the market aren't prepared because they lack a fundamental knowledge about capital. So in this chapter I'm going to present a primer on what every budding entrepreneur and founder needs to know about capital so you can have as much information as possible before beginning your capital (ad)venture.

What is capital?

For our purposes here, *business capital* is the term used to describe money invested in the business. In other words, financial backing. While most people invest money, some make a personal investment of time in a business. However, the time the entrepreneur puts into his business is not considered capital. It is called sweat equity. Only cash investments increase business capital.

Where do I get capital?

Regardless of the particular legal structure a business uses, there are two basic sources: debt and equity. Debt refers to the money borrowed by a business; equity refers to money invested in the business by its owner(s). Making a profit also provides equity capital.

There are three general sources of business capital: personal investment by the owners, outside investors—which would include government grants and local economic development authorities as well as business incubators—and shares in a company. All three options have pros and cons, but all share the main risk: the loss of money invested in the start-up if it doesn't make a profit and fails.

What is an accredited investor?

By definition an accredited investor has a special status under financial regulation laws. To be considered an accredited investor you must either have 1) an annual earned income exceeding $200,000 (or $300,000 when combined with a spouse) during each of the previous two full calendar years, with a reasonable expectation of the same income for the current year or 2) you must have a net worth greater than $1 million (either by yourself or combined with a spouse).

Before starting the process of raising money, due diligence about federal and state regulations regarding investors is imperative.

What is working capital?

Working capital is a company's current assets minus the amount of its current liabilities. It is a financial measure that calculates whether a company has enough liquid assets to pay its bills that will be due in a year. When a company has an excess of current assets, it can , on the other hand, for day-to-day operations.

Current assets include cash, inventory, accounts receivable, and marketable securities, are resources a company owns that can be used for business operations or converted into cash within a year. Current liabilities comprise the money a company owes, such as accounts payable, short-term loans, and accrued expenses that are due for payment within a year.

Having positive working capital can be a positive sign of the company's short-term financial health because that means it has enough liquid assets to pay off short-term bills and to internally finance the growth of their business. Negative working capital means assets aren't being used effectively, and a company may face a liquidity crisis. Even if a company has a lot invested in fixed assets, it will face financial challenges if liabilities come due too soon. This can lead to late payments to creditors and vendors, which in turn can hurt your young company's credit rating.

What is the best use of capital?

Business capital can be used for anything you need to run and grow your business. This includes inventory and equipment purchases (machinery, computers, vehicles); expansion to open a new location, build onto an existing location, add more parking, etc.), hiring and employee training; the unexpected (extreme weather, equipment failure, vehicle breakdown, quality control issues); other business expenses (rent, utilities, etc.).

How do I determine the amount of capital I need?

Investors always want to know how and why you need the capital you're asking for because they don't want to part with their money unless it's for specific, valid needs. So when you present your business plan, explain clearly what the money will be used for, how it will benefit your start-up, and how the business will earn a rate of return. And be specific. Don't just say $10,000 for office expenses. Itemize it: $1,500 for computers; $500 for two chairs and two desks; $6500 for the lease's first/last/deposit; and $1500 for IT.

Use of proceeds will show exactly where every dollar goes. Investors like transparency when it comes to your spending, especially if they don't know you. The investor will glean a lot about you by the way you plan to spend money.

Investors have a finely-tuned bullshit meter, so be honest. Just make sure your expenditures are necessary and not ego-driven. The only reason to spend $1,000 on an executive chair instead of $150 for a comfortable desk chair is image, ego, or narcissism, which could cause you to lose credibility. Investors like frugality. Most of them are hard-nosed professionals who expect you to show spending discipline.

And your initial funding has to cover more than just start-up costs. You also need operating capital, so be sure to include those costs in your financial projections. Make sure to give yourself plenty of time to show profitability in your business plan. That will increase your operating capital needs, and you want that cushion just in case things don't go your way. Most companies go out of business because they run out of money, and part of that could be because the entrepreneur didn't create enough of a capital cushion upfront.

Securing as much capital as possible is a typical, understandable impulse. But make sure you have a purpose for all the money you are asking for. Having too much can cause you to lose focus or give you a false sense of security, A well-thought-out business plan that itemizes your growth milestones over the next year or two will help you determine what you need. If you are choosing to obtain equity capital, get the right amount but no more, or you may cause unnecessary dilution.

What is a return on invested capital?

ROIC measures the percentage return that investors in a company are earning from their invested capital. The ratio shows how efficiently a company is using the investors' funds to generate income. However, ROIC is used mainly for assessing companies in industries that invest a large amount of capital, such as oil gas companies, semiconductor chip manufacturers, and even food conglomerates. So mostly this metric does not apply to start-ups looking for their first round of funding.

What is start-up valuation

Valuation simply means a company's perceived worth. For a start-up, valuation is based on other factors, including:

- customer traction; the more customers, the better
- reputation; investors love a winner. Someone like serial entrepreneur like Mark Cuban is going to get more benefit of the valuation doubt—traction or no traction—than a newcomer with no track record.
- having a prototype
- distribution channel
- tapping into an emerging market

The term start-up refers to s specific time in a business's life. Former entrepreneur-turned-educator Steve Blank explains that a start-up ceases to be a start-up when it finds a business model that is scalable and repeatable and when most of its employees start to focus on executing that business model. When a business gets to that point of post-start-up maturity, valuation is typically a multiple of its earnings before interest, taxes, depreciation, and amortization—known as EBITDA.

What are some sources to secure capital?

There was a time in this country when if you needed money to start a business, you went to your local bank, and it was likely the manager knew you. That era of true community banks is largely long gone. And over the years, especially since the Great Recession in 2008, banks' lending policies have tightened considerably, forcing entrepreneurs and start-ups to seek other avenues for financing. Obviously, not every source of capital is appropriate for every start-up idea. An entrepreneur needs to choose the financing source that fully meets their needs. Here is a brief review of capital sources from the more traditional to the creative.

Friends and family. When in need, most people tend to turn toward those they are closest to. Entrepreneurs are no different, and many start-ups have gotten off the ground through investments by family and friends. An upside about getting money from relatives is that it typically comes with low, no, or deferred interest payments, whereas a bank would likely charge significant interest if you could even get a loan, which you probably couldn't. On the other hand, avoid the temptation to offer a piece of the company out of gratitude. Better to pay interest on the loan. There are limits for how many non-qualified investors you can have for a start-up and how much money you can take from them, so make sure you know the regulations before you proceed.

Selling assets. For those who don't want to be indebted to others, they can try to self-finance. If you don't have a hefty savings account, you can sell some assets to get cash. That can be anything worth money such as artwork, a second car, savings bonds, and jewelry. I've heard several successful owners say they took a second mortgage out on their house to finance their start-up. Being an entrepreneur comes with risk; just how much you're willing to put on the line is up to you. But again, the advantage of selling assets is that you won't owe interest on a loan or have to give up part of your company. On a personal note, if you are in a relationship where finances are intermingled, such as a marriage, risk level can become a stress point that could impact the business as well as your personal life. So proceed with caution.

Bank loans. With a solid business plan, you might be able to get a small business loan from a bank. There are two types of business loans. A secured loan requires collateral, often a house or some other item of value like a car. So if you fail to repay the loan, those assets might be seized by the bank. Unsecured loans by definition have no collateral; however, it's possible a bank might require personal guarantees that commits you to carry the note even if your start-up fails. Whether or not you get a bank business loan will largely depend on your FICO score, which reflects your creditworthiness. That will also determine your interest rate on the loan.

Angel investors. An angel investor is someone willing to invest in a start-up to get it off the ground or to help with expansion once it is growing. Angel investors generally ask for a higher rate of return than a more traditional lender would request, specifically, they will probably want a share of your business and to be involved in decision making. The upside is that most times, no collateral or personal guarantees are required.

Home equity loan. A second mortgage is a loan that involves a second lien on a property where the money is given as a lump sum. As with first loans, seconds can be a fixed-rate or adjustable-rate. A home equity loan is essentially a second mortgage structured as a line of credit rather than for a fixed-dollar amount, meaning you can borrow from the equity of your house as you need to, when you need to. Home equity lines of credit, commonly called HELOCs, are always adjustable rate.

Merchant cash advance. If you plan to accept credit and debit cards for payment in your business, you can consider a merchant cash advance, which is financing given to businesses against their future credit and debit card sales. The advantage of this type of capital is that the lender collects a certain percentage of the credit and debit card sales, meaning that if the sales are low, he will take a low amount, and if the sales are high, he will take a higher percentage. It also does not come with interest rates since it is not technically considered a loan.

Invoice factoring. Sometimes called an invoice advance, with this type of capital, the lender grants the entrepreneur money against future payment of customers' invoices. One upside of this type of agreement is that the lender does not charge interest. A big downside is that if your clients fail to pay their invoices on time, you could end up losing the service provider.

Credit cards. With credit card companies lining up to send you cards, anyone with a decent credit score can accrue a lot of plastic credit. And that becomes a very easy source of capital, whether it's for buying goods or getting cash advances, and many entrepreneurs use credit cards to help finance their start-ups. The advantage of cards is that they're less expensive and more immediate than merchant cash advances, invoice factoring, and equity. But the obvious danger with credit cards is how quickly the interest can accrue if you only make minimum payments. So the quicker you can pay off the balance, the better your company—and your credit rating—will be. When using this method, however, you should be careful not to default on payments since the interest rates and cost on the cards build up very quickly.

Government grants. Various agencies of the US government offer grants to entrepreneurs with research-related start-up ideas that address a significant problem and that have strong commercial potential. And because it's a grant, the money is yours to keep, meaning you do not have to pay it back—one reason why they are more difficult to get. A word of caution: grants are structured various ways, and it is important to protect your intellectual property prior to taking a grant, or you may find the government owns what you developed with their funds.

Crowdfunding. The power of the people. Sites like Kickstarter provide entrepreneurs a platform to market their start-up idea and raise funds by supportive strangers who donate cash in exchange for various tiered perks, such as receiving one of the first produced products. As with a grant, the money is for the entrepreneur to keep. Similar to crowdfunding is online peer-to-peer lending sites like Lending Club that match entrepreneurs who need loans with people who are willing to extend the loans to them at an interest rate. After you register and the site's intermediary checks your credit report, potential lenders bid on your loan. The intermediary chooses the lender who's offered the lowest interest rate.

Microloans. Since getting loans from banks has become difficult, many entrepreneurs are looking into microloans from government agencies such as the Small Business Administration. The loans are relatively small—say, mid-five figures—but the interest rates are low. And it's a process. A credit card comes within a week; the process for an SBA microloan can take months and in most cases require guarantees.

Finance companies. Finance companies can provide loans to small business owners. As a rule it is easier to qualify for a finance company, but they also charge uniformly high-interest rates. And they are not tightly regulated so go this route at your peril.

Private equity. Private equity fund refers to an unregistered investment vehicle where investors combine their money for investment purposes.

How is private equity different from venture capital?

Some people confuse private equity with venture capital because they both refer to firms that invest in companies and exit through selling their investments in equity financing, such as initial public offerings (IPOs). But there are significant differences in how these two types of funding work.

VCs invest in industries that require heavy initial investments like energy conservation, high technology, etc. Private equity invests in all types of industries.

Private equity is an investment in the later stage of a company's development that are made in firms not publicly listed on any stock exchange. Venture Capital refers to the financing of early start-ups by investors seeking high-growth potential.

Entrepreneurs need to know the difference so they don't waste their time and others' time by trying to get capital from the wrong kind of investor.

What are some common myths about private equity?

The first is that private equity is a win-lose game—investors win and entrepreneurs lose. This is the common complaint of people who made bad choices. Maybe they didn't read the contract they signed, or they were too lazy to do their due diligence, or there was some other error of judgment that caused them to ultimately lose control of their enterprise. According to this myth, private investors will make off with the value of your company—perhaps buying at a low price and cutting you out of the eventual rewards—that you'd earn from going public or selling to another company.

It's important to remember that private equity investors only make money if the value of your company appreciates. And in most cases the entrepreneur retains a substantial interest in the business. It's also important to remember it's in the investor's best interest to help you grow your company and increase its value. So if the investor wins, the entrepreneur wins. That's win-win.

The second myth is that valuations are the only consideration when you're shopping the deal. Valuation is certainly an important consideration. You want to get a fair price when you sell your company; however, it's equally important to partner with an investor who shares your goals and who will work with you to achieve them. When you focus exclusively on valuation, you risk ending up with a partner who doesn't understand your company, your growth strategies, or your industry.

For example, let's say you sell your company to an investor whose expectations for your business are unrealistically high. You may obtain a good price for your company, but that relationship is likely to sour as the business fails to meet the investor's expectations. On the other hand, an investor with a more nuanced understanding of your company would work with you to increase its value in a realistic and sustainable way.

A third myth is that private equity investors don't add value because they haven't been in an operating role. This may be true in some cases but should be avoided as a generalization. Most financiers and professional investors I know have ample experience with operating issues. Also, though they don't usually try to micromanage portfolio companies; they can look at the operation from an objective perspective and add value by challenging management to think outside the box. Investors who have backed many different companies at rapid growth stages can recognize patterns that may not be obvious to the management team. They may have a network of relationships that can also assist companies in recruiting talent at the board and management level. They can often help companies explore strategic partnerships with other firms.

Another common myth is that taking private equity money means you lose control of your company because of sharks and other predators looking for a quick kill and smelling desperation. It can also stem from a person who is so determined to get their idea to market that they will accept any terms offered.

As an entrepreneur, you cannot abdicate your responsibility for the sake of expedience. Nobody is forcing you to take a deal and surrender control. I have found that the people who recount horror stories of how they had to take a back seat to an investor almost always did one of the following things. They either did not contact more than a few investors or took the first deal that was offered to them (laziness or jumping the gun out of worry it will be the only offer); they sold more of their interest in order to gain access to some quick money (desperation); or the entrepreneur exhausted all of their available resources and needed to cover the demands of his creditors (mismanagement).

The reality is that if you take on a minority investment, you can continue to control your company, make all operating decisions and having the ultimate say over strategic issues. It is my experience that the majority of investors do not want to run your company. They are busy running their own. Selling less than half of your company leaves you in charge while providing liquidity to you and other early shareholders.

Lastly, there's a belief that private equity investors are only interested in your exit strategy. That ignores some basic realities about investing. When a private equity firm invests in your company, they do expect to exit their investment within the next five to seven years. Since the firm has limited partners (LPs) who expect liquidity at some point, they can't hold their investment forever.

However, this doesn't mean that you will have to sell your company or take it public. Alternatives might include recapitalizing the company with bank debt, swapping out one investor with a new private equity investor, or raising capital from a strategic partner, often a non-financial sponsor. In any event, your private equity partner has a vested interest in growing your company over the next several years up to the exit event.

Their goal during this period is the same as yours: to increase the value of your company by helping you grow and expand the business.

Whether or not to take on private equity financing is a complex decision, requiring in-depth analysis of your personal and business goals, the market environment, and the financing options available. Focusing on these important considerations and putting these misconceptions to rest will help you make the right decision.

Should I seek venture capital funding?

That is a question without a quick answer. So in the next chapter, I'll go over the pros and cons of the current state of venture capital in America.

Chapter 5

To VC or Not to VC,
That's the Real Question

You are not the victim of the world, but rather the master of your own destiny. It is your choices and decisions that determine your destiny.

—Roy T. Bennett

One of the biggest decisions an entrepreneur faces is how to fund their start-up. While there are a variety of options as I discussed in the last chapter, for most founders it comes down to a choice between funding it themselves or going after venture capital. There is no simple answer, so it's not an easy decision.

The Upside of Bootstrapping

Bootstrapping means starting a new business without any external funding. The first advantage is not having to spend the time looking for investors, which can be a long process, and avoiding debt that can become an albatross if you don't make revenue fast enough. Instead you can use the time to concentrate on starting your business.

Entrepreneurs that bootstrap their start-ups use their own savings, credits cards, a second mortgage, or even proceeds from selling their home to provide the cash they need to get the business running and generating revenue. It's also not uncommon for entrepreneurs to keep their day job and work on their start-up in the evenings and on weekends.

Unless the entrepreneur happens to be wealthy, bootstrapping typically means a lot of sacrifices and significant sweat equity, especially in the beginning. Having limited funds forces you to stay focused on priorities and to make every dollar count. That may not seem like a positive at first glance, but over the long haul it will serve a founder well to develop careful money-managing skills, so you learn to maintain cash flow and don't overextend for unnecessary expenses.

Bootstrapped companies need a business model that will produce cash immediately, so it forces you to focus on how to make money, rather than how to spend it. That's easier to do when self-funded because you don't have investors impatient to start seeing a return on their money. Founders can dramatically increase their odds of long-term success by tempering their desire for instant gratification with some strategic financial restraint and discipline.

While it may seem like most start-ups are equity or venture-funded, in reality there are a lot of thriving companies that were bootstrapped, so don't think it's a detriment to success. Just as self-funding can instill smart money habits, it can also hone your problem-solving skills. Not having VC-type funds to throw at problems hoping something sticks, forces you to think creatively to come up with efficient solutions. In other words you are more apt to find less conventional answers to conventional problems. Some of the most innovative ideas occur when you back is against the wall. It's human nature to put in only as much effort as we need to; bootstrapping forces us to kick our efforts into a higher gear.

Not everybody is naturally cut out to be an entrepreneur, and self-funding is a good way to develop the constitution to emotionally handle the inherent ups and downs that are inevitable for any start-up. When a shipment is missed wiping out your cash flow, do you lose it or get so stressed you feel like you're going to implode? Or do you vent with a couple of choice curses then calmly figure out how to solve the problem? Running a start-up is stressful, and bootstrapping means you've put everything on the line, so it makes you develop the focus to work under pressure. Again, these are lessons that will pay dividends down the road.

For most entrepreneurs, the biggest benefit of bootstrapping is that they retain complete control of their company. If you don't take money from someone else, then nobody can tell you how to run your start-up, pressure you to ramp up before you or the company is ready. While you might not have the funding you would have going the VC route, what you will have is control and the right to make decisions that you feel are right without any outside interference. Too many founders that kind of independence is priceless.

Overall, bootstrapped companies are more effective at making constant course corrections, honing their business model, and constructing a strong foundation for consistent, sustainable growth. It's not uncommon for a business to change directions early on. Pivoting is easy when you're the sole owner of a business; when you have other investors like VCs ... not so much.

The Downside of Bootstrapping

The most obvious challenge of bootstrapping is working with limited funds, which gives you less room for error. Launching a start-up with your own funds means putting a profit plan in place as early as possible so you won't run out of money. And if your first plan doesn't work out the way you anticipated, you may not have the available cash to quickly pivot, which can hurt the growth of your business.

Another downside is one of perception. Self-funded start-ups can seem less important or not as validated as one flush with money from a VC, which presumably shows they have vetted you and your idea and have faith in both. Building a trusted brand in the eyes of consumers and other businesses may take longer when bootstrapping. Similarly, fewer resources can make it more difficult to keep up with your competitors in areas like marketing or advertising.

Lastly, not having deep cash reserves limits the amount of inventory or materials you can buy. And generally speaking, the larger the order, the lower the unit price. That in turn can allow competitors with deep pockets to sell their goods or service at a lower price point.

The Pros of VC … If You Can Get It

I meet hundreds of entrepreneurs and management teams looking for funding every year. People from all walks of life. Some very smart and others as dumb as a rock. They ask my opinion regarding their respective companies and if I think they'd be a good fit for some of our friends in the VC community for funding and growing their businesses. It all depends on the kind of entrepreneurs they are, the chemistry involved, what kind of company you want, and what your ultimate goals are.

The right outside investments can impact your start-up in positive ways. More cash reserves can immediately help overcome growth constraints caused by cash-flow challenges. It can also help you expand product and service offerings as well as acquire new partners. Taking the time to secure funding before building out your start-up can keep you from worrying about cash reserves so you can devote all your energies to creating a successful business.

While all that sounds great, before seeking VC money you need to determine if your idea is VC material. As a rule the types of businesses that venture capitalists want to fund are those with runaway potential that can produce huge returns. If you don't envision your business growing one hundred times in size, your start-up probably won't generate much interest. So generally businesses like restaurants, retail shops, a photography studio, and other small businesses that are not particularly scalable are not a good VC match.

According to *Forbes*, VCs follow two rules of thumb when looking for potential investments: Your market is worth at least $1 billion, and you can grow to $100 million in revenue and higher. VCs want ideas that are unique, have the potential to explode, and (supposedly) solve a problem essential to consumers. If your business doesn't check those boxes, you'll likely need to bootstrap or find an alternative source of funding. The problem is that what VCs say are important ideas or who they designate as top entrepreneurs are often based on faulty criteria, mainly geography.

People in the Valley, I find, believe in the myth that theirs is an efficient free-market economy of investment and that attempting to direct the entrepreneurial energy will kill it. This is laughable. The system is explicitly set up to direct entrepreneurial attention in ways extremely non-free. The entire region is wired to the capricious opinions of a few key people, who drive not only their own investments but via imitation, the money of lazier thinkers. Even if these people were 1000x geniuses with wonderful intentions for the world and preternatural ability to direct money in the right ways, there would still be a huge shortfall in the diversity of intelligence needed to make the money they control truly smart money. The money may be smarter than average investor Wall Street money, but it is nowhere near as smart as it could be.

A very simple measure of this is simply the high degree of localization of investment. Ghemawat in World 3.0 tracks liquidity and global flow of venture capital and estimates that the lion's share of investment happens within twenty miles or so of the investor. This happens because the investors mitigate the risks of their own limited knowledge by only investing in companies that set up shop locally, down the street. To get the money, entrepreneurs flood to the location of the money rather than the location of the markets/problems to be solved.

Some justify this by pointing to the advantages of high concentrations of talent. While this is certainly valuable, there is a very high cost paid in not being close to the problems and market opportunities. For example, people who have the market intelligence to solve water management problems are not going to emerge out of water-rich Northern California. They are going to emerge in Southern California, Nevada, and Arizona. So simply creating a technology that lowers the geographic distance risks of investment would be a huge plus. If a Silicon Valley VC firm could invest in an Africa-based entrepreneur with only 10x the risk of investing in a University Ave. firm instead of 1000x, money flows would change dramatically.

The misutilization of talent is so extreme I would rather invest in an average hustler and a non-10-x engineer team who are near an actual important market/problem than in a 10x super-star team in Palo Alto. Sure the latter would execute far more brilliantly and with all the latest technical tricks. But they are at a far higher risk of solving the wrong problem and then struggling to find a market. We are reaching diminishing returns from investing in the right team in the wrong place. Investing in even mediocre teams in the right place should provide good returns by comparison, on problems that actually matter and map to interesting markets.

The Value and Risks of VCs

VC money can either take your company to the next level or can tear it apart. It is not an easy decision and ultimately depends largely on your personal appetite for risk and the business you're considering. The value is evident when looking at the following factors:

Resources. You've got to really look at the resources you have available to compete. Certain types of businesses—such as those in the renewable energy, biotech, and telecom industries—may require significant amounts of capital just to compete. Without it they're basically doomed from the start.

The ability to scale quickly. Fast-growth businesses can certainly get by without VC funding in the beginning but will eventually need more serious capital to take things to the next level. And it's difficult to think strategically about the long-term viability of the business when you have short-term financial pressures. So if you want to quickly become a national or international player in a given industry, VC money might be the way to go.

Connections and expertise. The right VC firms not only give you access to their checkbooks, they make their Rolodexes and industry experience available as well. For entrepreneurs, it is all about smart versus dumb money. The key is accepting money from VC firms that can bring strategic partnerships, unique expertise, and key management skills.

Okay, that's looking at VC money in an ideal world. But there are also considerable practical risks. First and foremost, in a first-round of investing, a VC will want some ownership of your company, often 15 to 20 percent. In later rounds it can get as high as 70 percent.

In addition to sacrificing equity, taking a VC investment means ceding a certain amount of day-to-day managerial discretion. VCs bring their own blueprints for success—another way of saying preconceived notions about how you should be doing things. So unless you've negotiated autonomy into your agreement, it's hard to say no to their ideas since they're the ones paying the bills. And if your business model is as good as you think it is, you may be unnecessarily forfeiting a significant share of future profits by taking funding now.

If you want a small piece of a big pie, take the money; if not, stick to bootstrapping your business till you reach a critical mass. You will have much more leverage when dealing with the private equity/VC community in the future.

The next risk is that VC firms don't necessarily have your and your company's best interests at heart for the long run. They want what's best for their bottom line on their own timetable. These divergent opinions may not only lead to declining efficiency but also could create an unnecessarily hostile working environment. So I would advise to carefully evaluate your needs. VC interest does not guarantee success, so another funding source like a small business loan might meet your needs at a lower cost.

And as mentioned before, a start-up team with too much capital may fail to develop the bootstrapping skills necessary to achieve long-term growth. An abundance of capital tends to dull the business mind. There is the tendency to hire too fast, pursue too many unvalidated ideas, and spend on non-strategic elements of the business. Also, when too much of your attention is monopolized by outside sources— such as a hands-on VC whose ideas don't necessarily mesh with your own—your company's day-to-day operations might suffer, leading to mistakes that cost you in terms of both your company's bottom line and reputation.

VCs will also expect to have input on how your start-up is managed and its direction. And many venture capitalists insist on recovering their cash within a period of three years, which can lead to poor decisions.

I am often asked if VC money alone can make a start-up successful. You must understand that venture capital is a first step, but it's never enough on its own. Judging from how most VCs fund more losers than winners, there are plenty of examples that attest to that. But I really believe it all depends on the type of business you are in.

In consumer Internet entities, VC lets you defer revenues, maximize users, and go for the viral effect. This worked quite well for Facebook, Google, Instagram, etc. Basically, if you can defer revenues and become a top 100 to 200 website, then the result is outstanding. But if VC money can't get you to be a top-8400 website, then forget about it altogether.

Business Internet entities let you scale more quickly by creating, chasing, and closing longer and lower ROI opportunities. The rule of thumb here is that you should try to recover your sales and marketing expenses on a customer by the first year. It's a good model but only works if you have the capital to fuel the engine. Otherwise once you add in all the other costs, you'll be bankrupt. So if you have significant sales and marketing expense, you'll likely be significantly handicapped in how quickly you can expand and grow without capital. That means with business Internet start-ups, if VC money can't meaningfully accelerate your growth to a high level and you can't see a way for that growth to compound, you should pass.

Look at it this way; if you take capital to begin that business, your investor is now going to have a say in every major decision you make regarding the business. Now let's say that someone wants to acquire your business for $5 million; you'd make a nice profit if you had not taken professional funding. However, your investor is likely going to want to make more of a return on their investment—or they'll end up taking much of that $5 million buyout based on their investment.

However, if taking the capital is the only thing that will move your business forward or if it will shorten the amount of time from now to reaching your goals, it may definitely be worth it. It's very much an individual decision based on your own goals. More money usually increases the chances of success, but there are thousands of other factors like poor management, no market fit, better competitors, etc., that can cause your start-up to fail, regardless of the money it has. It really comes down to how effectively the money is used, not how much you can get, that determines your success.

With less capital it's harder to scale, and that's actually a good thing. Scaling too soon forces you to grow and make decisions before your company is ready. Expectations are lower with less capital. And your milestones will be more manageable. Also, larger amounts of capital lead to unnecessary dilution at a lower valuation. Conversely, smaller amounts of capital allow you to preserve more ownership and can lead to higher valuation in future rounds.

The sooner you sell equity, the more it will cost you in the long run in loss of leverage as well as dilution. Instead I always advise start-ups to do everything they can to get their company off the ground and build traction prior to raising funds.

The takeaway from all this is that while by definition, VC is used to help a business grow and develop, there are never any guarantees. So tread thoughtfully and carefully before taking the VC plunge.

Chapter 6

What Venture Capitalists Won't Tell You

We are so accustomed to disguise ourselves to others, that in the end, we become disguised to ourselves.

—François de La Rochefoucauld

T o hear venture capitalists tell it, they aren't too different from entrepreneurs. They build great companies. They create jobs. In short, they feel the entrepreneur's pain. But for an entrepreneur to build a decent relationship with a VC, they need to understand just how different the two of them really are.

It is a fact of business life that compared to entrepreneurs, VCs have different loyalties, sometimes diametrically opposed interests, and a lot less at stake. Having been interacting with VCs for about three decades now, I have learned some important truths venture capitalists won't tell entrepreneurs.

Experienced VCs know that less than 1 percent of venture-backed technology start-ups will ever achieve a $1billion market capitalization. So they seek category potential, not current company performance, meaning they look for companies leveraging technology to build and dominate new market categories. If the category is big enough and the category king is dominant enough, current valuation is almost irrelevant.

As a result, legendary VCs study category potential, not current total available market and ask the question: *Can this become a giant new space? Can this founding team summon the balls, brains, and bucks to become the company that dominates this giant new category?* If the answer to both is yes, they start drafting term sheets. If the answer is no, you are dead in the water.

For as much as venture capital is in the news, you'd think these high-end investors had funded half the successful businesses in the country and beyond. But the reality is much narrower. VC is a very select form of financing. In the United States, which is the most active VC market in the world, only about one thousand businesses get new financing per year. That's .025 percent of the approximate four million businesses started in the United States each year.

Obviously, not all those are VC quality to begin with, but even so, it's still only a minute percent of companies seeking VC funding get it. The odds get even worse for entrepreneurs in Canada, Europe, or Asia. There's actually a lot more money to be found in family offices and the pockets of high-net-worth individuals. But venture capitalists won't advertise that. They want to perpetuate its huge mindshare and mythology.

Similarly, they don't want to admit that as an industry, venture capital's return on investment is seriously behind that of the public stock market. From 2007 to 2016 the average internal rate of return for American venture capital funds was 6.1 percent annually. During the same time, the Nasdaq rose 10.3 percent annually, and the Dow Jones Industrial Average returned 8.6 percent a year. Given that VCs skim the first 20 percent of annual venture fund profits off the top, people who invest in them have begun to wonder what they were paying for. If you intend to make the right decisions, it's time to wake up, smell the coffee, and recognize facts from fiction.

The pension and stock fund managers who invest in VCs are called limited partners. The very top VCs don't have to wine-and-dine their limited partners; they just pick up checks. But most VCs have to sell up just like you do. In fact, they have to do more of it in some ways, because they probably have fifteen to twenty limited partners, whereas most entrepreneurs usually only have one to four VCs.

It almost seems counterintuitive, but as individual investors, venture capitalists aren't that diversified and don't do very many deals. VC firms as entities, though, get pretty diversified. But the average VC partner only does one to two deals a year. While that might be more diversified than you as a founder, relatively speaking it's not as diversified as you'd think. So their deals really need to work because ironically they don't really want to take much risk, which is why you need to have your ducks completely in a row when you pitch to a VC.

As with most businesses, there are large and small VC firms, and you should research which size firm you want to approach. Generally speaking, the smaller the fund, 1) the more aligned with you they are, 2) they make less in fees and more on the carry, and 3) more practically, they can't keep up with the dilution. Because they can't write the large checks, they need someone else to. And small VCs also need to buy a lot for a small amount. If they can only invest $2 to $3 million and want to own 15 to 20 percent, that pretty much puts a cap on small VC valuation potential.

By contrast, not only can large VCs write a big check, they want to. But the return has to be huge to impact the fund. Fire the CEO, fire the founders, dilute you with nothing—they could not care less. But they'll give you more money to go big.

When it comes to VC size, one is not better than the other; both have pros and cons. Just pick the one that best matches how you want to grow.

Lastly, here are some facts to consider if you're thinking of going the VC route:

- Very few VCs invest in the seed stage. Those that do tend to invest mainly in their extended networks.
- The chance of getting VC investment through a cold contact is infinitesimal. At the very least, get a warm introduction; otherwise, don't even try.
- Regardless of what they claim on their web sites and at conferences, each partner and firm has specific investment criteria and stages. Ask people who have worked with them or are familiar with how they do business to find out what they are. There is an art to it, but they also have their criteria, and they have metrics; they're just not telling you.

So next time you go pitching a venture capitalist, remember those facts and most importantly make sure you pick the right partner. But again, also understand that VC money isn't a gateway to the entrepreneurial promised land.

According to the *Harvard Business Review*, "VC firms position themselves as supporters, financiers, and even instigators for the past twenty years. However, the industry itself has been void of innovation for the past twenty years."

Despite declining returns, venture capital, structured funds, partner payouts, and the raising capital process are the same as they were two decades ago. VCs decide which companies to invest in based off of a formula that by their own admission has a success rate of 9 percent. To me, that kind of hubris makes no sense in any context.

There is no shortage of venture capital in the world. It's just not available to entrepreneurs when they need it the most: from idea to *aha*. At aha your potential is evident, and financing is easier to get. So why is there such a capital gap from idea to take off, especially outside Silicon Valley? Consider these facts:

- Risk is very high; about 80 percent of ventures fail or break even
- Risk is higher before aha because the potential is not proven. Many ventures may be competing for the same opportunity on the same emerging trend. Only one or two are likely to survive and dominate. The rest will fail.
- The winning ventures need to make up for the losses and provide the desired return in an early stage VC portfolio. This means early-stage VCs need home runs. The home runs are in Silicon Valley. Early-stage VCs have not done well outside Silicon Valley.
- Due to the high risk, about 97 percent of VC is provided after aha, and my guess is that a lot of the remaining 3 percent is provided to repeat entrepreneurs who have succeeded with their earlier ventures. Entrepreneurs need to have skills and know the strategies to bridge the capital gap (i.e., to grow without VC from idea to take off).
- The capital gap is real. Entrepreneurs need to know how to bridge the opportunity gap, strategy gap, and leadership gap if they want to find venture capital, control it, and use it to create wealth and control it.

My take is that smart financiers wait until aha before they climb aboard the bandwagon. Entrepreneurs need to bridge the capital gap from idea to aha with expertise, not capital or sophisticated market research.

How Venture Capitalists Are Killing Companies

To recognize how venture capitalists are killing companies, you need to understand how venture capitalists work internally. VC firms typically have managers who we come to think of as investors because they sign the checks. They are also referred to as general partners (GPs)

The LPs, on the other hand, are the investors in the venture capital firms themselves. They are called *limited* because they don't actually invest in VC firms or start-up companies; they invest in an individual partnership which raised one or more funds from LPs.

Most of these limited partners are massive financial institutions that work with venture capital on a diversified investment strategy capacity. And once a fund is raised by investors, the money is committed for the life of the fund. The VC then takes the limited partner's money and uses it to invest in a bunch of stock. There are strict rules on what VC funds can do with the money because they are limited partnerships.

Venture capitalists make money from successful exits, and original investments are returned to the limited partners. After that, 80 percent of profits are paid to the limited partners, while 20 percent of the profits are retained by the general partners.

This system is killing start-ups because ultimately, the fund structure of VCs isn't ideal for start-ups. Everything about the VC structure is misaligned, from the structure to skills to timeline. Most VC funds have eight or ten years to identify companies, nurture their teams, and eventually take them to exit. Only then can they return money to their limited partners. The problem with this structure is that it takes most start-ups longer than five or eight years to grow to a meaningful size for a big public—and big money—exit. Historically most start-ups need at least ten years or more to reach a size considered stable. That math doesn't work. There's an obvious disconnect because there's no way a VC can get the benefit until the end because they have to return money to their limited partners before they made any real big money.

And there's the rub. It's also where it gets ugly. Worried that they won't make any real money, VC's start telling the start-up to become something that's worth selling to someone else. To convince the entrepreneur, the VCs engage in meaningless and often expensive campaigns or a merger with another portfolio that's ill-advised. And if that doesn't work and it's getting close to year seven, they'll look into selling the company to anyone willing to pay a decent price, regardless of what this means for the start-up. If none of those tactics work, then it's *too bad, so sad* for the businesses that either get pushed to getting bought or going public. The only other option is choosing to go broke.

Ultimately, what kills companies is the demand for continued growth. VCs are bound by their contracts to return the stock to their limited partners. One might be charitable and think the VCs have no choice and their hands are tied. Or one might see it for what it is: they're not very bright, and instead of taking better care of the start-up and nurturing it to become something incredible over the course of the fund's life, they suck the life and potential out of it.

Maybe if VCs started to focus on meaningful exits rather than fast ones, we'd see more innovation thrive and stop seeing the demise of otherwise brilliant start-ups that were just a means to an end.

Chapter 7
The Rules of Negotiation

Let us never negotiate out of fear. But let us never fear to negotiate.
—John Fitzgerald Kennedy

t's been said that it's not what you know, but who you know. People do business with people, and it's essential that entrepreneurs understand this going into any venture. Some of my greatest ideas and projects went nowhere because I didn't know the right people—yet. More so, complicated deals went ever so smoothly simply because I knew the person in charge.

Connections Are Paramount

"At the end of the day, and no matter what technological miracles are conceived, people do business with people. The greatest deals in the world are sealed by a simple handshake, and some are broken over simple personal animosity."

In my thirty-year business career, this famous quote that my father kept repeating to me ever since I was a teenager, is probably the single most potent business lesson that I have learned.

My firm, Blackhawk Partners, has carefully been building our contact network the world over. I humbly believe that the network we have built is not only incredibly extensive and far-reaching globally, but is also one of the company's greatest assets, way ahead of any physical asset we own or ever will. The same goes for sound advice; it's a priceless asset when professionally and effectively conveyed.

Good advice and targeted connections can make all the difference and oftentimes do. That's why I love advising and backing people and companies to the best of my knowledge and reach out to the sharpest minds all across the world. A snowball effect occurs: the more I do, the more I learn, the more fascinating people I meet, and the more effective I become.

Just as important as having good connections is, I avoid, like the plague, negative people who emanate negative vibes. I have a knack for detecting falsehood and those who dish it out from a mile away.

Art of the Deal; the Rules of Engagement

I meet thousands of people a year—both online and offline—and I'm frankly flabbergasted at how well-educated and supposedly highly-connected people are so awkward during business engagements. For the most part, they think that just by soliciting a person online—on LinkedIn, another social network or even through a referral—that they are now at equal footing and can sell you anything they want.

Then, when you face them with reality, they become very frustrated, act weird because they didn't get what they were looking for and drop you as fast as they met you. Welcome to the age of shallowness, stupidity, and the soundbite.

Let me share with you a few priceless tips in the hope that you'll learn how one really gets ahead in life and can make things happen

Listen First and Stop Talking

Listening is the single most important life skill in professional and personal relationships. Ernest Hemingway said, "When people talk, listen completely. Most people never listen." It's sad but true: Most people have their own agenda and are too busy talking (or waiting to talk) to listen to you attentively. If you, unlike most people, can truly listen with empathy, then people will like you—and eventually help you get what you want.

Help Others

It's perhaps another paradox, but it works:

When you want something from someone, instead of asking for it, help that person get what he or she wants. If you don't know what he or she wants, then simply ask: *How can I help you?*

Since so many people are out to only help themselves, when you genuinely seek to help others succeed in attaining their goals and realizing their dreams, you'll stand out. And those people you genuinely help will in turn fight to help you in succeeding. Help others first, without expecting anything—and the returns will be enormous.

Be Yourself

Oprah Winfrey stated, "I had no idea that being your authentic self could make me as rich as I've become. If I had, I'd have done it a lot earlier."

Professionals, especially of an older generation, tend to have a tough time with authenticity and transparency in the workplace. People, especially men, tend to have a tough time being vulnerable, especially with people they don't know well. Many also aren't sure how much to reveal online, or at work, or to people they've just met. But, hard as these choices may be, authenticity, transparency, and vulnerability all breed trust. And when people trust you, they'll do anything for you. Open up to people and take a chance —you'll be rewarded.

Tell, Don't Sell

As important as it is to listen and help others, in order to get what you want, you've eventually got to tell people what that is. Nobody wants to be sold to—so, whether it's a product, service, idea, or yourself that you're trying to sell—give up on selling. Instead, focus on telling a great story—captivating your audience, bringing to life what the future will bring, and painting a great picture of what will happen if you get what you want. When you get good at storytelling, people want to be a part of that story—and they want to help others become part of that story too.

Inject Passion Everywhere

Passion is contagious, but so is lack of passion. If you're not passionate about what you're talking about, why should someone else care? If you want something, you must be more excited and dedicated to it than anyone else. If you're not passionate about it, maybe it's not really that important to you. You don't need to be bouncing off the walls to convince someone of something. You just need to reveal your true passion, in a way that's genuine for you.

Surprise and Delight Others

This is really very simple. When you surprise and delight others, not only do you make them happy, you remind them that you're the type of person who might surprise and delight them soon again. Some classic examples: bringing home flowers to your wife for no reason; telling a customer his order will arrive next week but then overnighting it; etc. If you go out of your way to make an experience, especially when people least expect it, you will get huge results over time.

Apologize When You Make a Mistake

Say *I'm sorry* when you make a mistake and *thank you* as much as possible. These words are so simple, yet so often people overlook the importance of saying them. Everyone makes mistakes, and everyone knows that. It's not when you make a mistake that's a problem; it's when you make a mistake and are too proud or embarrassed to be vulnerable, fess up, and apologize. Just say *I'm sorry* and let another person forgive you, so you can move on, and eventually get what you want. Conversely, sincere gratitude is a powerful emotion to convey and opens many doors.

The Art of the Deal; Rules of Negotiation

Not only do I engage with many people constantly, I negotiate with hundreds of people a year—both online and offline—with customers, suppliers, investors, or would-be employees.

I can humbly say I learned over the years to negotiate like a true master, though we all sometimes get into trouble when something careless just slips out.

Here are a few priceless tips to avoid if you are really keen on improving your negotiation skills:

Avoid the Word *Between*

It often feels reasonable—and therefore like progress—to throw out a range. With a customer, that may mean saying: *I can do this for between $10,000 and $15,000.* With a potential hire, you could be tempted to say: *You can start between April 1 and April 15.* But that word *between* tends to be tantamount to a concession, and any shrewd negotiator with whom you deal will swiftly zero-in on the cheaper price or the later deadline. In other words, you will find that by saying the word *between* you will automatically have conceded ground without extracting anything in return.

"I Think We're Close"

We've all experienced deal fatigue: The moment when you want so badly to complete a deal that you signal to the other side that you are ready to settle on the details and move forward. The problem with arriving at this crossroads, and announcing you're there is that you have just indicated that you value simply reaching an agreement over getting what you actually want.

A skilled negotiator on the other side may well use this moment as an opportunity to stall, and thus negotiate further concessions. Unless you actually face extreme time pressure, you shouldn't be the party to point out that the clock is loudly ticking in the background. Create a situation in which your counterpart is as eager to finalize the negotiation (or, better yet: more eager) than you are!

"Why Don't You Throw Out a Number?"

There are differing schools of thought on this, and many people believe you should never be the first person in a negotiation to quote a price. Let the other side start the bidding, the thinking goes, and they will be forced to show their hands, which will provide you with an advantage. But some research indicates that the result of a negotiation is often closer to what the first mover proposed than to the number the other party had in mind; the first number uttered in a negotiation (so long as it is not ridiculous) has the effect of anchoring the conversation. And one's role in the negotiation can matter, too. In my experience, the final outcome of a negotiation is affected by whether the buyer or the seller makes the first offer. Specifically, when a seller makes the first offer, the final settlement price tends to be higher than when the buyer makes the first offer.

&*%$# You

The savviest negotiators take nothing personally; they are impervious to criticism and impossible to fluster. And because they seem unmoved by the whole situation and unimpressed with the stakes involved, they have a way of unnerving less-experienced counterparts. This can be an effective weapon when used against entrepreneurs because entrepreneurs tend to take every aspect of their businesses very personally.

Entrepreneurs often style themselves as frank, no-nonsense individuals, and they can at times have thin skin. But whenever you negotiate, remember that it pays to stay calm, to never show that an absurdly low counter-offer or an annoying stalling tactic has upset you. Use your equanimity to unnerve the person who is negotiating with you. And if he or she becomes angry or peeved, don't take the bait to strike back. Just take heart: You've grabbed the emotional advantage in the situation. Now go close that deal.

After all is said and done, in life you don't get what you deserve; you get what you negotiate.

PART II
DON'T LET FAILURE HAPPEN TO YOU

Too often entrepreneurs are reactive to the challenges inherent when building a company, meaning they wait for a calamity to happen then try to respond, the start-up equivalent to swimming upstream. The most successful founders are proactive. This section discusses how to best prepare for the hurdles inherent in building a business.

Chapter 8

Pitching to Investors

Investors are people with more money than time.
Employees are people with more time than money.
Entrepreneurs are simply the seductive go-betweens.
Start-ups are business experiments performed with other
people's money.

—Antonio García Martínez

I am approached by hundreds of entrepreneurs every year, pitching me their respective businesses. Some are very polished and focused, others amazingly ineffective and convoluted. You will usually only get one chance to pitch your business to a particular investor, so you better make it as professional and compelling as possible. Here are some general guidelines I would encourage all entrepreneurs to follow if they want to improve their chances of connecting with investors.

Don't oversell; let the idea sell itself. I understand that most entrepreneurs are passionate about their start-up idea, but please don't bullshit me or sound like an infomercial. We have accumulated more data than you can imagine to call your bluff even before we've met. So you won't do yourself any favors by adopting an overconfident, know-it-all persona who sounds like a cross between a sleazy lawyer and a used car salesman. Just be yourself, be accurate, and be honest; don't even think about making up a padded résumé.

Lay out the framework. Simple and direct is best. Don't beat around the bush. Give concise, focused answers.

Assume I know nothing about your business. It is always a challenge to find the right balance when pitching your idea. It's like the Goldilocks dilemma: you don't want to give too much or too little; you want to give just the right amount of information. You're not going to have a lot of time to pitch; make it both complete and succinct so the investor knows what your product does, why it's relevant, and what problem it solves in the market.

There's an old saying that you should be able to give a complete pitch in the time it takes to ride an elevator. While you'll have more time than that, it's a good adage to remember.

Be aware of body language. Scientists say that more than 90 percent of all communication is non-verbal. Half the time we're not even aware of the signals we're giving with our body language, but you'd better learn fast. Rolling your eyes, audible sighs, crossing your arms, bouncing your leg, all of those are easy-to-read tells. If you disagree or don't like a question a potential investor asks or their attitude, be mindful not to show annoyance or frustration through your body language.

Personally, I have found that thinking positive thoughts when I disagree with someone keeps me from tensing up or displaying any outward sign of unrest. If your mind is projecting positive thoughts, your body language follows suit. Never let them see you sweat; that immediately gives them the upper hand.

Tell me something I don't know. Too many entrepreneurs come and tell potential investors stories about the industry, their exponential growth potential, and how great they are. This is of no real interest to the investors whatsoever. What they are most interested in is how you are going to execute and create obscene wealth for them. Anything short of that is white noise. Very few entrepreneurs—only the real killers—are able to flesh out a unique value proposition, and those are the ones investors will line up to fund.

Yes, you do have competition. A sure-fire way to lose the interest of an investor is to claim that your business idea has no competition. While it may be true that no other company sells a product substantially similar to yours, that doesn't translate to a lack of competition. Any substitute product, process, or service that satisfies the same need is a competitive solution. To say otherwise reveals either a lack of market research or ignorance on your part.

While you might mean that your new product, process, or service is so unique, proprietary, or innovative that it will corner the market, saying something has no competition actually can be construed to show that there's no perceived need for your start-up or if there is a need, the market is too risky, undesirable, or minuscule to be profitable, making it unattractive for a VC. Better to identify the competition and explain how you will overtake the market share.

Also, be respectful of your competition. Disparaging other companies will detract more from your business plan more than it adds. It's uncalled for, lacks class, and reveals an emotional immaturity. And from that, the investor will make judgments about you as a manager and leader. Stay on point. Offer information that shows you have a thorough understanding of the competitive landscape.

Keep sweat equity to yourself. Don't confuse believing in your business enough to make personal sacrifices to sustain its survival with investing in your start-up. While forgone salary represents an economic cost of the venture to an entrepreneur, it is not a cash-money financial investment into the business. If you have input a significant amount, that's something to include in your business plan because if you haven't put your own money into the venture, don't expect me to.

Keep it realistic. Don't use hyperbole in estimating your market or how much market share you project you'll capture. Incorrectly sizing the market will tell the investors you lack either 1) the knowledge to assess who would buy the product or 2) the integrity to delimit this statistic accurately. If it's the former, the investor will think you are either too lazy or too stupid to succeed. If it's the latter, they will simply not want to be in business with you. Either way, they are not going to fund your plan. You have to approach business as a war, and the only way to win is to be armed with more and better intelligence.

And here's another reality. No matter what numbers you put in your plan, the investor is going to have their analysts and intelligence network confirm them. If there is a variation of more than a few percentage points, that's a red flag that you might not be smart enough to know how to take an investment and build it into a healthy return. So pay attention to details and be honest.

Here is a sobering fact: four out of five entrepreneurs fail to raise the capital they need, and their great business idea turns into a lost opportunity. So here is a taste of the questions you better be prepared to answer.

Why is the requested capital necessary for your business to succeed?

Knowing why you are raising the capital is as important to an investor as knowing what you are raising capital for. Your investor is going to have a pretty good idea of what is required for certain businesses to succeed. And if you are asking them to fund you and become partners, that gives them the right and the obligation to know what you are or will be doing with the money.

A serious investor is not interested in funding lifestyle entrepreneurs who have somehow convinced themselves that in order to be taken seriously in their business, they have to have a penthouse overlooking South Beach, a chauffeured limousine, and a private jet. The investor is looking to fund a performance entrepreneur who leases space in an office park, drives an appropriate vehicle, and if necessary, has a membership with a service providing fractional ownership of a corporate jet. A good investor isn't opposed to utilizing all of the tools necessary to turn your venture into a success. But you have to show then you understand concepts like opportunity cost, risk and return, and deferred reward. The trappings of success come to those who have earned them—not to those who are living on someone else's dime.

Outline exactly why you need capital and how it will benefit your business venture; investors don't want to give up their money for nothing. If you need the capital because your business cannot operate without it, say so. If you need it to expand, tell them that. Have an end game. Outline what you intend to achieve and your measure of success. Yes, they want a return on investment, but they will also consider whether your business can generate better results with their capital invested than it would without it.

How have you been funded to date?

Investors primarily want to know the business' current total expenses and how you have funded your business so far. Generally, they don't care to hear details of when and how you began incurring business expenses.

How much of your own money have you invested?

The answer very little is probably a deal-breaker. After all, if you don't believe enough in your business to risk a reasonable amount of your own assets, why should anyone else? On the other hand, answering: *Everything I have and then some* will also raise red flags because your business should not be an albatross. Investors expect to see control and stability, not a sinking ship.

What are your start-up expenses, and how have they been covered?

Businesses commonly incur significant debts during their start-up phase, and investors want to know how much red ink is on the table. Don't try to hide your debt; just be able to precisely detail what the expenses paid for and the steps you've taken to control those expenses.

Showing the start-up phase has been well managed, with expenses efficiently controlled while income accumulated, strengthens the appeal of your investment opportunity. Also, be ready to back up the information you provide in your financial data.

How will you make money?

Investors are not in it for charity. Your business plan must answer this question in detail. Your methods for generating a profit are fundamental to whatever investment deals you construct. Since investors want more than the return of their initial investment, how a business is poised to make money over the long term is a crucial aspect. Investors want a hook that will reel in customers and revenue.

When your business interests are focused on a single set of products or services, you need to be realistic about the degree of competition you can survive. Presenting an idea that cannot be easily copied shows you have clearly thought through how your business idea will function in the real world and how you will stave off competitors. The easier it is to copy or replicate your product or service, the more competition you will have, sooner rather than later. Enough competition, especially by someone who improves on your original idea, could put you out of business before the investors recoup their money. Prognosis: no deal.

Keep in mind that pitching investors is a process that requires preparation, data, vision, and honesty. And even if an investor passes on this particular start-up, don't burn the bridge. Keep them periodically apprised on your progress because they very well might be interested in a later round of funding.

Chapter 9

The Curse of Incompetent Entrepreneurs/CEOs

One of the biggest sicknesses this world has is expectation. We all expect other people to be a certain way or to do a certain thing. Most people, they spend their whole lives under the wants of other people.

— **Eric Shonkwiler**

F or many people the biggest upside of being an entrepreneur is that they get to be their own boss. For many start-ups, the biggest downside is that the entrepreneur is their own boss.

Just as I know some excellent C-level executives who would be abysmal entrepreneurs, not every entrepreneur is born to be a CEO. Most shouldn't get anywhere near an executive suite. The notion that

76

you are automatically qualified to run a growing company simply because you founded the business is either arrogance, stupidity, or both. While some entrepreneurs are rock stars who can do both, it's rare.

The brutal truth is most first-time entrepreneurs simply do not possess the experience, business maturity, or mindset to be an effective CEO of their company straight out of the gate—or in some cases even after the second or third race. It's an error in judgment that probably torpedoes more start-up businesses than any other. And the mistakes made are so predictable because they are the result of incompetent execution. Unfortunately, most entrepreneurs only learn the hard way—in retrospect—by having a business fail. If you want to improve your odds, learn from others' miscues now so you can avoid them with your own start-up.

One of the more fundamental blunders is not appreciating how much a company's needs will change as it grows. When you found a business, you are an entrepreneur looking to get funding, develop your product or service, find a customer base, and secure a foothold in the market. You are looking to either introduce something completely new (Ted Turner launching the first basic cable channel CNN) or innovate an existing type of product or technology (Steve Jobs's iPhone).

But once the company becomes established, it's time to switch gears to a CEO mindset. Instead of focusing on developing the product and making consumers aware of it, you need to think about how to grow and expand the business to make it sustainable. A CEO is responsible for creating and implementing the strategic direction of a company, everything from marketing and branding to financial management. The CEO has to manage in the present while developing a vision for the future. Entrepreneurs obsess on the small details of their product or service while a CEO needs to keep sight of the big picture. Entrepreneurs often fly by the seat of their pants when developing a start-up and are willing to take risks. CEOs are focused on growing profits along with sales to make the company—and investors—money.

It all boils down to this: entrepreneurs see themselves as innovators and disruptors; CEOs need to be leaders and visionaries. The inability to make the leap from the former to the latter is at the heart of the CEO incompetence of most start-up founders. In my experience there are two types of mistakes: those that are part of the growing pains any company goes through and those that are borne from arrogance or ego.

One of the more interesting aspects of sudden wealth is how quickly it can make people careless about spending. You need to be skilled in sustaining cash flow, but without a strong business plan, something a CEO develops, you won't necessarily know where the next dollar is coming from. Debt is a constant issue. Knowing when to spend money for expansion or equipment upgrades also requires skill.

Entrepreneur CEOs can avoid the hubris and arrogance that often accompanies new-found revenue by remembering these simple rules: acquiring more company profits does not equal acquiring more managerial expertise; debt is a dangerous tool, especially in the hands of the inexperienced; assets are not the same as income, wealth is not the same as cash flow, spending is not the same as investing; and thinking: *My company is making money; therefore, I must know what I'm doing* is a recipe for disaster when not backed up with actual knowledge and experience.

I am flabbergasted that so many smart entrepreneurs are so inept at managing money. It's one thing to introduce a new product or service and find the money start rolling in. It's quite another to know how to best utilize that money. Many end up blowing it all up faster than they acquired it, and the company implodes. Michael O'Donnell was one of the lucky ones who had the good sense to recognize his lack of good sense in time.

In his early twenties O'Donnell founded Cave Tools, which sells a line of barbecue accessories. After his business took off, he named himself CEO. "I started my company within four months of graduating from college. So I had to learn every area of business myself through trial and error—mostly error." That included managing money.

He had used debt financing to rapidly grow the company. "The bank gave me a $100,000 line of credit at 5 percent interest," he recalls. "I thought: *Okay, if I put a dollar in my company, will it spit out more than $1.05?* The answer was yes. So I worked on the systems in my company so I could spend as much of the 100K as the business could handle, paid all the interest, and got back to debt-free. After that year the company was much bigger with zero debt and had about ten products that were all generating cash."

Michael admits that when starting out, he was motivated to hit a seven-figure revenue mark because that was his vision for success.

"I was young, and people don't take you seriously, and that was really my ego speaking. So in 2016 I decided that since I had borrowed all that money in 2015 and done so well, in 2016 I was going to do it again, but double down on it. And that year we did bring in way more money with $1.8 million in revenue. But I only ended up with a $30,000 salary that year. I had officially taken $50,000, but I had to put back about $20,000 because we had no cash flow and bad debt. And I was devastated because I'd had so much money available to me, but I made stupid, dumb decisions."

One of the realities for start-ups and established companies alike is the need for cash flow. What had been a boon in 2015 had been a bust in 2016. He says the difference was his mindset.

"When you don't have a lot of money, you are more careful. Let's say you have $1,000 to work with. If you have to make a $100 spending decision, you're going to be pretty tight with that; you're going to make sure it's worth it. But when you have $200,000 to work with, a $100 spending decision now seems like nothing. So instead of starting out with maybe one or two thousand units of a product to test the market and then make modifications to make it better before manufacturing more, there was so much money available that I was starting out with five- and ten-thousand-unit orders because I thought I was on top of the world, and nothing could stop me. But then we had quality control issues. And quality control issues on a ten-thousand-unit order is a lot different than a quality control issue on just a two-thousand-unit order."

After that experience Michael decided in 2017 that what really mattered was the bottom line of the company. "I put my ego aside, and now we follow a system I learned about that ensures the business runs incredibly profitably by flipping the script and taking profit first and apportioning what's left for expenses. In 2017 we did $2.5 million, and we're incredibly profitable."

But he admits every step along the way was a constant learning process, especially being open to suggestions that can help his business or him as an executive.

Michael recognized your new-found wealth is not an automatic ongoing revenue stream. You never know what the future holds no matter how much you plan, so the importance of living within your means is critical whether you have $500 in the bank or $500 million. Insolvency occurs when your liabilities exceed your assets and cash flow, regardless of how many zeros are on either side of the balance sheet.

Another problem for many entrepreneurs-turned-CEOs is making the tough decisions. When you started out, still living in your parents' basement, if you made the decision to keep working on a new product that everyone else said was a non-starter, nobody was affected but you—and your long-suffering parents. But when you have a growing company with employees and investors to consider, that kind of indulgence can land you back in the basement. It's not just about you anymore. You have to consider the big picture now. So if something isn't working, cut your losses and move on—today.

Ben Lerer, cofounder and CEO of Thrillist Media Group, says, "During the last nine years building Thrillist Media, of course there were times when I realized pieces of the business or certain strategies weren't working. My approach is always to admit as early as possible that the approach is failing and work to resolve the situation. I've had to make some really tough decisions, but ultimately, I think the best companies are those that can recognize when something isn't going right and fix it, without letting it drag on."

In other words, the CEO has to make tough decisions based on the company's needs, values, and goals as opposed to their personal whims and wishes. But that doesn't mean that the CEO should be making every decision big and small. Some entrepreneurs think that being a company's CEO means being involved with everything, mostly because when building a start-up, they wear all the hats.

But that doesn't work once the company is up and running. Anyone who clings to the *If you want something done, do it yourself* philosophy, will ultimately doom the company because what they are really doing is getting in the way and usually just slowing down progress. Don't be a moron. Surround yourself with really smart, trustworthy people and start delegating. You're not running a mom-and-pop business, so the best decision you can make is to surround yourself with smart financiers and advisors you can trust and who have done it before. Pick their brains and start listening.

And not to just the professionals. You'll do yourself a huge favor by focusing on making your team and your customers happy. Talk to them honestly and ask them how they think you could improve. Carefully evaluate what they say. It's especially important to get input from people who haven't invested the same time and effort you did getting the start-up off the ground because they will be more objective, which will help you make those hard decisions, like letting go of an employee who's underperforming.

Having trusted advisors who are straight shooters is also a way to get honest feedback. They will be there to let you know when you're making decisions based on ego instead of what's best for the company. Having a little humility will give you the flexibility to create a business that can thrive in good times and survive the bad.

Growing a company is a marathon that requires patience, dedication, knowledge, good decision-making, vision, and the ability to see the big picture. I'm not saying entrepreneurs can't evolve into a savvy CEO. You can if you are willing to put in the time and effort up front to learn and develop the necessary skill-sets that will enable you to lead your company to sustainable success. Everyone makes mistakes—every entrepreneur, every business leader, every employee. The mark of a competent CEO isn't that they are perfect—that's impossible—but that they have developed the humility, wisdom, and foresight to turn mistakes into opportunities.

Lastly, entrepreneurs that recognize they need someone else to be CEO to move the business forward are the entrepreneurs that should be invested in. Acknowledging shortcomings is profoundly wise and simply good business because it gives the start-up the best chance for success.

Chapter 10
Don't Be a Statistic

The most important thing to know about statistics is that you don't have to be a statistic.

—Adam Smith

The hundreds of entrepreneurs I meet every year go from one extreme to the other. Some are true mavericks and game-changers; others are arrogant and ignorant. What differentiates a killer entrepreneur from the chaff is how they operate, regardless of what product they are offering. They understand that developing their product or service means nothing if you don't develop a solid business infrastructure around it. Without that, you'll simply be another statistic of a failed start-up.

One of the most important decisions an entrepreneur has to make is hiring. Let me give you some advice: be extremely careful about hiring in general, especially if you plan on hiring family. Working with relatives or close friends can be a difficult dynamic that doesn't work for most people, even though it might seem like a fantastic idea when you're starting out. But for most of you, it's best to avoid that complication.

Instead, invest the time to hire smart people that intimidate you with their knowledge, drive, and passion. It's critical to surround yourself with complementary skill-sets. It may sound obvious, but you need people who possess strength where you are weak, and you need to check your ego at the door. If you are not the most organized person in the world, surround yourself with people who are. It will take you and each of your employees to make your business a success.

Your criteria for hiring can depend on what your business is. Some start-ups require people with specialized technological or financial expertise when they hit the ground running. But if you are starting a solar panel installation company, you may be more interested in an applicant's energy and willingness to learn than their past experience because you want to train them to your particular installation process.

While a résumé is important, there's a lot more to consider than just what's written on a piece of paper. I have interviewed people who have a great résumé, but they just don't have *it*, that special quality. No matter how good a résumé looks, you need to determine whether the applicant is going to fit in with your company culture and be the high-performing individual you are looking for.

At Blackhawk I don't seek out people who have the shiniest diplomas. Anyone who applies for a job at Blackhawk will have to meet and interview with me first. Then if I'm satisfied that the candidates meet some basic screens, they go and interview with my other partners. If my partners and I collectively agree that the candidate is a fit, only then do we have them meet with the HR Department.

During the interview I only ask them one question, and from their response to that one question, I'll have a pretty good sense of what's in their gut.

The question is: *What pisses you off?*

Nine out of ten will answer: *Oh, there's this, there's that …* and they are immediately disqualified because they are trying to please me and fit into a perceived mold. They have been conditioned to conform. The one who responds with something like: *What kind of a question is that?* is the one that makes it through the hiring process. It's telling me that this candidate has an independent mind. That this candidate has the potential to be a leader who can and will think for themselves, not someone who will say whatever it takes to please their potential future boss. Those are the ones I would like to see it make it and join our team. All the other stuff can be taught, but you cannot teach character. I want people who are going to challenge me, not people who are going to try to be nice and play along because that's what they read in a textbook at their business school.

Many entrepreneurs swear by the virtual office, which is where you hire people who work for you remotely via the Internet. So you might have an executive assistant in Michigan, a sales rep in Chicago, and you are based in New York. That might work for some online companies, but most businesses need their employees present or at least nearby. You need to have oversight, and that's very difficult to do when someone is thousands of miles away so hire locally at least in the beginning.

Being a founder means you have to run your shop professionally and be a boss, not one of the guys or a best friend. You have to run the business with an iron fist and be on top of everything. My lifelong mantra? *Have an iron fist in a velvet glove.* Discipline is key; without that your start-up will go nowhere. Just like children, employees need clearly defined boundaries. They also need to know their responsibilities and your expectations as well as how much advancement they can achieve in your company.

Lastly, if it doesn't work out, rip off the band-aid immediately. A disruptive, dishonest, or disloyal employee can not only create an uncomfortable or hostile working environment, they can also spread discord to other employees. You must cut out the cancer and fire them at once. Nobody is truly indispensable. And the ultimate cost to keep a bad employee could be your start-up failing.

Putting Customers First

From day one, listen to your customers. It sounds simple, yet so many business owners think they know what's best. Your customers know best, and your customers are the people who will help build your brand and your business simply by word-of-mouth. With social media so prevalent in our society, it's easy to hear what your customers are saying. Just ask; then make sure you follow through. A founder has no excuse not to be in continuous communication with their customers.

Top of mind should be: *What's going to make my customers happy?* Most importantly, know their respective histories in every way—company history, personal history, marketing history, investing history, etc. Then use it creatively. Instead of sending out Christmas cookies, donate money to every customer's favorite charity.

The best customers don't just use your product or service. They are fans, which means they will remain loyal and follow your business as it grows. That is how Richard Branson built a billion-dollar business without venture capital: by building his customer base and creating a legion of fans.

How Brand Improves Profitability

Cash flow is crucial to every business but especially for a start-up, so work toward profitability immediately. That's more important than spending time trying to find investors whose money is expensive because of what it will cost you down the road. Being profitable gives you options and agility. But profitability doesn't mean gouging your customers, so price your product or serving fairly. If your product is good and you sell it for a small margin, more people will buy it. Then later you can increase the price of upgrades, new products, and value-added services and people will happily pay because by then they are not just buying the product; they are buying your brand.

One of the most common mistakes that start-ups make is not focusing on building a brand starting on day one. It is vital to get your company name out there into the public eye, so your target customer gets to know your brand. MySpace gave local bands free pages, knowing their fans would check the new service out. Then those fans virally announcing the news about this fantastic new service called MySpace. A year later Mark Zuckerberg made sure every student at Harvard knew about Facebook, which would become a viral sensation and eventually trample MySpace. The best marketing and advertisement is a brand spreading by word of mouth; in fact, it's priceless, which is why your initial lowball pricing doesn't matter.

All great brands have a distinctive brand promise. *The Ultimate Driving Machine* (BMW). *To bring inspiration and innovation to every athlete in the world* (Nike). *Think different* (Apple). *Your package will get there overnight. Guaranteed* (FedEx). Even the United States Postal Service understood the value of a brand promise: *Neither snow nor rain nor heat nor gloom of night stays these couriers from the swift completion of their appointed rounds.*

All those promises state why consumers should choose that brand as well as make clear their primary value proposition. The most effective brand promises are creative and courageous—the bolder, the better. Be disruptive, challenge the status quo, and connect with consumers on an emotional level. Be a showman. Be creative.

Be dependable. When a brand delivers on a promise, they cement customer loyalty.

A brand promise should define a clear and simple idea and translate into a story. How does the product change their lives when they buy it? Does it improve them in any way? What's going to be different? By defining your relationship with your audience with a story, your brand promise then takes the wheel.

A final suggestion. I always tell people never to use a public relations firm or some other bloodsucking investor relations firm. You are the best PR for your company, especially at a start-up's early stages, because it's your vision that is the foundation for your brand and its promise. Nobody can do that better than you.

Knowledge Is More than Power; It's Money

Surveys have found that the majority of entrepreneurs rely more on gut feelings to make decisions than they do on a conscious, informed analysis of a situation. Even though they may be highly analytical and like to accumulate data, their actual decisions are usually based on what feels right. Even though they may gather as much information as possible and consult with their team, in the end they make decisions based on their gut or intuition.

Perhaps. But I am convinced their gut is impacted by the knowledge they have acquired. They may believe it's all intuition, but I would argue intuition is in part your subconscious mind analyzing all the facts and figures you have fed it, which is why gathering information and intel is crucial to making decisions. It is the essence of it. For example, if you understand the demographic changes occurring, your gut will tell you it's time to start refocusing where your marketing dollars go.

Talking head pundits on news programs are only going to make you stupid, not smarter. Newspapers, financial reports, trade publications, government data, think tank data—you need to read this stuff regularly to understand what is going on. Every week I read at least two hundred pages of intel prepared by my SWAT team. You cannot imagine how your decision-making process—and your intuition—will improve once you have all that information laid out for you. So every single day you must educate yourself.

Embrace Your Competition

Many entrepreneurs fret about having competition. I welcome it. Competition is good because it shows you have a decent business model. It helps you judge progress. It shows that other people value the space you are in. So to succeed you simply have to outperform the competition. That is also good because accepting that challenge turns you into a killer.

In business the only constant is change. So your fiercest competitor today might be your partner or acquiring buyer tomorrow. So treating them like a hated enemy is self-defeating and not smart business. Instead, build bridges. Invite them to lunch to get to know them. Smart entrepreneurs will push their ego aside and let the other person do most of the talking because that's how you learn what the other guy is doing. That's more than a conversation; that's first-hand intel.

Caveat emptor: just don't discuss pricing or carving up markets with your competitor if you are offering similar products and/or services. It could land you in jail.

Focus on Focus

Unless you're one of the privileged few who get VC or private equity money, you'll be like most entrepreneurs, wearing all the hats in the early days of your start-up. Even after your business starts growing, it may seem like there are never enough hours in the day. People often talk about time management, but I think the more underrated, often overlooked, but essential skill is learning to focus. Specifically, knowing what to focus on, and when. The ability to keep the mind concentrated on the issues at hand and not allowing it to wander off can make or break your success in getting your business funded. Focus is the cessation of the modifications of the mind and is indispensable in business and in life.

Almost all entrepreneurs work hard, spending almost all their waking hours on building their business. But are they working as efficiently as possible? If you're not focused on the right things, you'll be the proud owner of a failed start-up. While everything may need your attention, somethings need it more. You have to focus on the right things in the right order, so the challenge is to determine what's really important *now*. That will remain the challenge as you move forward as well. Too many entrepreneurs waste precious time and energy on unnecessary tasks and a misguided pursuit of perfection. While you spend three days tinkering with your logo, the rest of your business can implode.

Some people have a natural gift for innately knowing what to focus on. Most people don't. So every day write down the top three things that your start-up needs that day, then rank them in order of priority.

The Intangibles

Focus, profitability, distribution, marketing, and competition are all vital elements to build a successful start-up. But there are also intangibles that can't be measured or taught such as enthusiasm, energy, and boldness. There might not be an algorithm to chart these traits out, but their importance is crystal clear and work like hell to keep them burning bright. Don't let a little success dull your inner fire.

Remember being poor enough so that you take nothing for granted. Remember making life decisions at the gas pump, remember sleeping on couches and sofas. Remember the feeling of hunger. Remember how it drives you. Remember so that you do not want to go back there again ever. Remember it so that you are not scared of losing it all. Remember so that you will be grateful for what you have. In my best moments of clairvoyance, I always go back to the thought that it is better to be young and hungry than old and fat (metaphorically speaking).

That is how you refuse to become another failed start-up statistic.

Chapter 11
Mistakes Are Opportunities

Remember the two benefits of failure. First, if you do fail, you learn what doesn't work; and second, the failure gives you the opportunity to try a new approach.

—Roger von Oech

When building a start-up, the life of an entrepreneur is largely spent solving problems, such as late orders, quality control, needing more staff, improving cash flow, and all the other daily issues that arise.

It is near impossible for any entrepreneur to realize their dream of owning their own business without having a team and mentors to help them to get their business on a sound footing. The team helps the entrepreneur to implement their vision by structuring the business plan into succinct, short-term goals and guaranteeing that targeted objectives are met, thus playing a decisive role in turning an aspiration into a reality.

While many entrepreneurs choose to find a co-founder, this can be a costly mistake. As the founder and CEO of a company, I can tell you that it is lonely at the top, and it is difficult to find a good sounding board for your ideas. A mentor can give you reassurance that you are on the right path with your ideas and share experience that you will not find in thousands of how to do bullshit business books. Mentors will encourage you and make it more likely that you succeed. Bill Gates had Warren Buffet as his mentor, Warren Buffet had Benjamin Graham, Mark Zuckerberg had Steve Jobs, and so on.

While most founders are mentally prepared to problem-solve what are essentially typical system and process matters, problems caused by their own mistakes can bring a start-up to a halt. Not because of the error itself, but because of the way the founder reacts to it. Some stubbornly refuse to own up to the mistake and start finger-pointing at others— the entrepreneurial equivalent of Nero fiddling while Rome burned—or they are so demoralized they are willing to walk away.

And to be sure, some mistakes can be fatal. If you grossly mishandle money by leasing an expensive office, buying a new car, and ordering a tailored wardrobe leaving nothing for actually running the business, or if your planned product does not work and you failed to have a Plan B. your budding enterprise will die a quick death. But while usually uncomfortable and occasionally embarrassing, most mistakes are far from lethal. In fact, they are often extremely valuable. The difference between a sustainable business and a floundering start-up isn't whether the entrepreneur avoids mistakes; it's how they react to the mistake, learn from it, and apply that lesson.

At the very least, making mistakes is the best way to learn. There's a reason the adage *You learn more from failure than success* has become a cliché—it is so true that it should be obvious. As is the saying: *If you're not making mistakes, you're not trying.* Everyone makes mistakes—every entrepreneur, every business leader, every employee. If you take a nosedive a hundred times, keep trying until you succeed.

One of the mistakes I made as a young man was thinking I had *arrived.* That was my mentality during crucial stretches of my twenties, to my detriment. Thinking you've 'achieved—whether you're talking about personal happiness, level of income, status, or whatever—is a static worldview and stunts your growth. I eventually came to terms with the fact that if you want to achieve, you can never stop trying; if you're not learning something every day, you're stagnating or regressing.

Steve Jobs, Bill Gates, Warren Buffet, and Jeff Bezos all made mistakes, and it only led to greater successes. The mark of a strong business isn't that it avoids failures—that is simply impossible—but that it has the wisdom to take full advantage of them.

It's incumbent on young entrepreneurs and experienced CEOs alike to let go of the pride that doesn't want you to admit that you're wrong. As Plato said, "The worst of all deception is self-deception." But it's a waste of time to wallow in guilt or shame. Your time is much better used, and your company much better served, coming up with a solid action plan that fixes it or at least minimizes the negative impacts of the mistake along with a strategy on how you can avoid such a problem in the future.

Behavioral economics tells us that humans in general are short-sighted by nature. We are hard-wired to seek out evidence that confirms what we already believe and to ignore evidence that contradicts it. We are also usually inherently overconfident. According to a study published in *Nature* magazine: "Some authors have suggested that … overconfidence—believing you are better than you are in reality—is advantageous because it serves to increase ambition, morale, resolve, persistence … which actually increases the probability of success."

Perhaps. But overconfidence also leads to a buffet of mistakes—faulty assessments, unrealistic expectations, business hubris, market bubbles, financial collapses, and policy failures—caused by tunnel vision and myopic judgments, especially by entrepreneurs who are often self-centered, and arrogant in addition to being overconfident. The great virtue of mistakes, whether by accident or design, is that they widen your range of experience and shrink your ego and thereby open you to discoveries you might not otherwise ever make.

History is full of such mistakes that led to discoveries, new opportunities, and unexpected successes. In the early 1960s a meteorologist at the Massachusetts Institute of Technology (MIT) named Edward Lorenz had completed an extensive number of weather system simulations and now wanted to repeat the experiment over a longer time frame. The computer model was based on a dozen variables such as temperature and wind speed, whose values could be depicted on graphs. Lorenz wanted to repeat a simulation he'd run earlier.

To his surprise and dismay, the second simulation diverged radically from what he was anticipating. He puzzled over it for days. Then Lorenz had his *eureka!* moment: he had rounded off one variable from .506127 to .506. That tiny alteration drastically transformed the entire pattern his program had produced, which covered more than two months of simulated weather.

On one hand the second simulation was a failure because he had mistakenly rounded off the data numbers. But that error led Lorenz to a far more significant discovery: in a complex system, minute changes in the initial inputs can cause massive changes at a later stage. That idea came to be known as the *butterfly effect* after Lorenz suggested that the flap of a butterfly's wings in China might ultimately cause a tornado in Kansas. The butterfly effect, one of the pillars of chaos theory, also suggested something else: forecasting the future can be nearly impossible.

What happened with Lorenz is an example of what I call a brilliant mistake, which has two components: something goes wrong far beyond the range of prior expectation, and new insights emerge whose benefits greatly exceed the mistake's cost. The former is necessary for the latter to occur, so ideally you want to increase the chance of both happening together.

Another example of that occurred in the late 1800s when pharmacist John Pemberton was trying to create a general pain reliever that would also ease headaches by combining coca leaves, cola nuts, and some other ingredients in a kettle in his backyard. One day his assistant mistakenly mixed the ingredients with carbonated water instead of plain tap water. But when Pemberton tasted it, he liked it and thought they might be able to sell it. They named their beverage Coca-Cola. The assistant's mistake turned into one of the world's largest companies.

What happened with Lorenz and Coke were inadvertent, unplanned mistakes. But in business many mistakes tend not to be accidents. Some happen through a lack of vision. Not that long ago the video rental business was booming, and no company was better known than Blockbuster. Then technology started elbowing its way into that industry with streaming services like Netflix. In 2000 Netflix made Blockbuster an offer: it would handle Blockbuster's online component, and Blockbuster could host its in-store component, which would eliminate the need for mailing DVDs. The meeting didn't go so well.

Former Netflix CFO Barry McCarthy later said, "They just about laughed us out of their office."

The Blockbuster brain trust simply didn't have the vision to see the potential of streaming services. Fast forward to 2018. The last Blockbuster store closed, and Netflix was a content, cultural, and streaming powerhouse. Mistakes of vision may be the most unforgiving because once you miss your window of opportunity, the rest of the market has not just caught up but passed you by.

Kodak was the poster child for this. Long before digital cameras became a mainstay in smartphones, a Kodak employee invented one of the first digital cameras in 1975, which the company patented. But Kodak wanted to protect their film business, so they put the technology under wraps rather than being at the forefront of an inevitable future.

In Vince Barabba's book *The Decision Loom: A Design for Interactive Decision-Making in Organizations*, Steve Sasson, the Kodak engineer who invented the digital camera, says, "It was filmless photography, so management's reaction was: *That's cute—but don't tell anyone about it.*"

Kodak's own internal research concluded digital was the coming trend but wouldn't reach critical mass for another decade. Rather than use that time to prepare a pivot strategy, the company leadership continued its focus on traditional film cameras. The irony was that George Eastman, who founded the company in 1880, had twice made such pivots that embraced cuttingedge, disruptive technology of the time, which helped him build Kodak into a global brand: first he had sacrificed his very successful dry-plate business in favor of roll film, then later embraced color film believing movies and consumer photography would move away from black and white film. At its peak, Kodak controlled 80 percent of the US photographic film market and half of the global market, employing sixty thousand people in the US alone.

George Eastman was a man of vision; Kodak's executives in the late twentieth century were not, and their mistake destroyed the company as we knew it. By the time Kodak finally pivoted, they couldn't secure a big enough piece of the market because they were too far behind and filed for bankruptcy in 2012. Today the company still exists but as a much smaller enterprise, with less than twenty thousand employees worldwide. Its revenue comes primarily from the nearly seven thousand patents it owns and it now also develops technologies used in digital imaging and touch screens. But what it could have been.

The other main type of mistakes are errors of judgment. Almost one hundred years after Coca-Cola was invented, it found itself losing market share to its arch-rival, Pepsi. Coke's market research determined people were developing a taste for sweeter flavors, and Pepsi was capitalizing on that trend. Even though the Coca-Cola brand was basically synonymous with soda, some genius executives decided to change the original formula and market the revised drink New Coke.

On April 23, 1985, New Coke was launched with a marketing blitz that included prime-time TV ads. Then-company Chairman Roberto C. Goizueta proclaimed New Coke was "smoother, rounder, yet bolder." The public begged to disagree. Angry consumers equated the company's actions to stomping on the American flag.

Coke lovers started hoarding cases of the original soda. In June 1985 *Newsweek* reported that opportunistic black marketeers were selling the original Coke for $30 a case—the equivalent of $70 in today's money. One Hollywood producer rented a wine cellar to hold a hundred cases old Coke he had bought.

Clearly, somebody had made a grave mistake in judgment.

On July 11 Coca-Cola started yanking New Coke from store shelves, and Coca-Cola Classic was reintroduced. In a profound understatement, company President Donald R. Keough said, "We did not understand the deep emotions of so many of our customers for Coca-Cola," and with that New Coke went down as one of the biggest blunders in business history.

Fortunately for them, Coca-Cola had the money and brand recognition to survive their mistake. More importantly, they quickly acknowledged their mistake and fixed it rather than stubbornly holding their ground. And they learned the valuable lesson of never underestimating the power of consumer attachment to a beloved brand.

The more you can normalize mistakes and embrace them as an opportunity, the more you will be able to leverage mistakes to your advantage. At my company I ask my partners to share their mistakes at a monthly meeting. At first they were reluctant to open up, but these confessionals have now become a favorite part of the session. The partner who presents the best mistake of the month gets a trophy. Initially the trophies stayed hidden in the desk drawer of the (un)lucky winner. But as everyone realized sharing mistakes was making them and the company better, people started placing the trophy on their desk all month, using it as a conversation starter with clients to explain how they transformed their mistakes into opportunities. It took time, but I managed to change the culture from one that hides mistakes to one that celebrates them, and our company reaped the benefits.

Many entrepreneurs worry that if they admit a mistake, their clients will abandon them, but history tells us it's more than likely they will appreciate your honesty and empathize. Consider this: former president John F. Kennedy was never more popular than he was after he flubbed the Bay of Pigs invasion in Cuba. Despite the political embarrassment it caused, JFK accepted full responsibility, which showed that he was not only human and fallible but also honest, forthright, and willing to shoulder the responsibilities of his office. Because Kennedy fell off his pedestal and dirtied himself but didn't pass the buck, people could identify with him and gave him credit for it.

Maintaining the respect of a client is the fundamental yardstick for measuring your success. Clients know that none of their suppliers is perfect. More to the point, clients do not expect perfection and will be suspicious if your company never makes a mistake. In my experience, I found that clients respect truthfulness, humility, and the ability of a supplier to say: *I'm sorry; I made a mistake. and I will fix it.*

Nobody means to make a mistake, whether inadvertent or an error of judgment but accepting that it will eventually happen enables you to develop a plan of action for when it does occur. (Most of the time people don't know they made a mistake in vision until it's too late to do much about it.) The first thing you must do is simply admit it and approach it as an opportunity to learn what not to do next time. Too often pride or fear—of ridicule, embarrassment, losing funding, alienating clients— prevents people from owning up to making a mistake, which only amplifies the problem. If I hadn't learned from my mistakes, I might have had a much different, less successful career.

On the other hand, while you might have to deal with the consequences of someone else's mistake and be responsible for it as their superior, you should not take the blame for it. You are not helping anyone or your business by covering for others. Just like refusing to accept responsibility for your own mistakes will keep you from improving, not making other own up will stifle their growth as well.

After realizing you've made a mistake, it is crucial you understand why it happened so that you can prevent a repeat. The more objective you can be, the more you will learn. The question for a founder is how do you empower people so that they will feel safe enough or compelled enough to own up to mistakes and be energized by the opportunity that mistake presents. I believe there are several ways to do it.

Build a culture. Empowerment will not happen if there is a culture that doesn't back it, one where challenges are thrown at people, and their perspective is accepted, and their efforts in handling the challenge are appreciated. Assure them they are doing a good job even if they fail. Help them do things that are one step ahead.

Leadership not only involves sincere respect for the rights and feelings of others, but also demands that workforces do the right thing and refrain from any behavior that might be harmful to themselves, co-workers and their company, or that might be viewed unfavorably by current or potential customers or by the public at large.

See yourself as a mentor. Give them the freedom to make decisions. Help them validate those decisions then let them take risks and learn from their mistakes and successes without micromanaging them. That will help them realize their true potential. And there is no greater feeling of empowerment than learning you have an ability to make a positive contribution to the world. That gives people even more incentive to see mistakes as an opportunity that will advance them on their journey.

Don't shoot the messenger. Nobody wants to hear bad news, but the only way to fix a problem is to know it exists. Just as you must create a culture where mistakes are seen as opportunities to improve, everyone needs to feel safe reporting bad news and understand it's their responsibility to do so because it can only better the company. Conversely, make it clear that there is no place on the team for anyone who seeks to cover up unfavorable developments out of fear it will reflect badly back on them.

Be a leader. A good friend of mine has enumerated the qualities of an entrepreneurial leader: Be moral. Be brave. Be a wholehearted person. Hold true to your focus. Listen and learn about each team member. Set the example of driving results. Show your intent to excite those around you. Be the epitome of team strength. Give your team the freedom to do their job. If you are committed to your team, you will realize their commitment in return. Stand on the principle that it is more important to be respected than to be popular. Acknowledge that your team needs to know you care about them individually. Demand that your people add value to the organization through their work and fulfill your end of the bargain by being truthful and keeping your standards high.

Lastly, *take the time to build trust* between you and them and encourage trust among your team. If you trust their actions and decisions, they will feel empowered and won't view a mistake as the end of their career.

A final word of caution. Yes, by and large people are willing to accept an honest mistake. But they are not willing to accept mistake after mistake after mistake. It's one thing if a mistake occurs because of circumstance or a miscalculation or the unexpected or inexperience; it's another if it's part of a pattern of carelessness or ineptitude or laziness. Then it becomes a choice, and those kinds of choices are one reason why so many start-ups fail.

Chapter 12

Leadership Skills That Will Grow Your Business

Success is not how high you have climbed, but how you make a positive difference to the world.

—Roy T. Bennett

To grow your business quickly and sustainably, you have to be prepared, be agile, be proactive, and be ethical. There are no shortcuts. There can be no shadiness. And from day one you need to lead by example.

There has long been a debate over whether great leaders are born or created. Regardless of how a leader develops, a common attribute of effective leaders is charisma, which is the ability to attract, charm, and influence people. It may seem like you either have charisma or don't, but psychologists have identified the main components of charisma including a personal and professional confidence that invites team members, peers, and the public to trust in their abilities and goals; exuberance; optimism; and a friendly voice. They inspire people with their determination and ability to produce results.

Charismatic people also have the skill of being mentally present. When they talk to someone, they aren't distracted checking their phones or glancing around the room. They look people in the eye, listen to what they are saying, and respond thoughtfully, which makes others feel noticed and appreciated. Those qualities build morale, help spur productivity among employees, and are also attractive to investors.

Being the center of attention is a useless leadership trait in itself. The ability to convert an audience's attention with a purpose, lesson, or other message is how a charismatic leader takes the reins and realizes the potential of a following. A mob accomplishes chaos, but an organization under the guidance of a focused leader produces achievements.

While charisma contributes to a leader's effectiveness, it's not a make-or-break necessity. Introverts can be effective leaders too. That's because leadership is a culmination of varied traits that taken together improve the ability to bring people together.

Histories, businesses, and societies around the globe are peppered with stories of great leaders who can rally teams to focus on goals, the betterment of lives, and successful ventures by relying on inherent and learned traits and skills such as the ability to communicate over many platforms. And by that I don't mean just sending messages; I mean effectively explaining ideas and goals. Be precise in your vocabulary and be detailed in your thoroughness because people aren't mind readers. And remember communication is a two-way skill. It's not just about holding court and listening to yourself talk; it's just as important to listen to feedback and others' ideas so you can constantly refine your company's goals as well as your own.

It is difficult to invest energy, time, or money in a person who has no goals. Leaders inspire others by demonstrating that they can set and achieve personal and organizational goals. Setting benchmarks provide a measuring stick that helps determine success. That said, goals are by definition aspirational. Missing a goal is not necessarily an indicator of failure. It can serve as motivation to work even harder or to come up with more effective strategies.

Authenticity Sells

I am frankly flabbergasted by the number of time-wasting bullshit artists there are in the business world. If you ever want to be considered a serious leader, stop trying to put on airs and just be yourself. If you don't believe me, believe Oprah Winfrey, who commented, "I had no idea that being your authentic self could make me as rich as I've become. If I had, I'd have done it a lot earlier."

I find that entrepreneurs who are older tend to have a tougher time with authenticity and transparency in the workplace. Men especially have a tougher time being vulnerable, especially with people they don't know well. But authenticity, transparency, and vulnerability each breed trust. And when employees and business associates trust you, they'll do anything for you. So open up and let your real self show through and you'll be rewarded. Adopt a persona and bear the consequences.

Smart vs. Dumb Money

Leadership requires a lot of practical knowledge and savvy, especially when it comes to finances and financing. For example, if you have multiple entities or people who want to invest money in your business, you need to determine which is the best option because not all money is worth taking. Smart money brings along the promise of help, while dumb money carries hidden harm.

Ask yourself these questions:

- Is this investor investing in your industry for the first time?
- Is this investor investing in a start-up company for the first time?
- Is this investor's lawyer in the start-up investment scene for the first time?
- Is your company's target market new to him?
- Is this his first time investing in a company trying to raise multiple rounds of funding?
- Does he insist on adding a non-dilution clause in your operating agreement? (A savvy investor never asks for this because everyone •dilutes when an investment is made)
- Is he asking for an equity stake that doesn't correlate with the funds they're giving you?
- Is he pressuring you to take the money by a specific time, not wanting to explain why?
- Does he insist on keeping CPAs and lawyers out of the investment discussion?
- Are his references and background impeccable?

If you answer yes to one or more of these questions, there's a good chance you're looking at dumb money.

A good rule of thumb is to choose your investors the same way you would choose your business partners. They need to have the resources that help you grow and expand, and they should bring something other than money to the table; it is essential to find investors who add immediate value to your business and not just your bank account. That will set the tone for how you will continue to grow it and help establish a healthy investment culture.

So when looking for smart money, your investor should provide: coaching and mentorship (when needed); an established network to help you grow your company; contacts to other accredited financiers; credibility based on their references and reputation; and skill-sets that your company lacks such as in sales, financial management, operations, computer programming, HR management, etc.

Another tip: even if some investor says they want to be silent partners, you'll still need to make a clear and documented agreement before you sign the papers. This will help you avoid any conflicts when the business starts to grow.

Learning to Read People

I meet with hundreds of entrepreneurs, financiers, and businessmen all year long. Some are smart and others amazingly dumb. But there is one type of person I find delusional—those who think they can get away with dishonesty or outright lies. If judging people on first impressions were an Olympic sport, they'd suspect me of using performance-enhancing drugs. Learning to differentiate the wheat from the chaff is a vital skill, especially for founders trying to establish a growing, sustainable business. Here is the process I use that will help sharpen your people-reading skills.

First, I start with small talk

Before you can tell whether someone is being dishonest, you need to get a sense of how they communicate during a normal, non-stressful conversation. Engage in small talk about some neutral topic like the weather, your favorite sports team, what kind of dog you have, etc., and watch their mannerisms. It's the same principle behind the questions they ask to start a lie detector test. You need a baseline that reflects truthful responses so you can eliminate potential tells such as foot-tapping or using a lot of verbal fillers such as uhm from regular idiosyncrasies. The best time to discern a baseline is when you're building rapport with people. And you don't need much more than five minutes to determine that baseline.

Listen carefully

Statement analysis can help you discern when someone isn't telling the truth. For instance, if you ask a yes or no question, the answer should actually contain the word yes or no. Answers like *absolutely* or *of course* could be a signal that they're either lying or don't understand what they are talking about. To drill down, at that point ask a follow-up question and listen carefully for the next answer. It should be short, simple, and to the point. People lying or being dishonest tend to overexplain. Also listen for defensiveness.

On the flip side, the liar may overcompensate with a lot of character references. Always check. You're likely to be surprised at what you find out. Most people don't either because they find it too time-consuming or think it is somehow intrusive. When it comes to your business, there is no such thing as intrusive. Business is war. If people don't open up, tell them to stop wasting your time.

Unfortunately, there is no proven way to detect a lie unequivocally, but there are some general tendencies that you may be able to detect. And often the way they act while they lie depends on the severity of the situation, who they're lying to, and how prepared they are to mask their nonverbal behaviors. A habitual liar doesn't fail the test immediately. It is only when they can't remember what they lied about last time that they are shown up. Wear them down by asking them the same question differently and see how they respond.

Maybe the last question you should ask is: *Did you tell me the truth when you answered all these questions? I am just looking for a yes or a no.* Surprisingly, some people will admit to a small fabrication, and you can get at the truth. If you're looking to hire someone who will be in a position of trust, it's imperative to know whether this person you're considering is truthful, so you can follow up with a particularly powerful question: *Why should I believe you?*

Here's the tricky part: Whatever answer you get first, don't accept it and ask a second time. *That didn't really answer my question—why should I believe you?* You won't know unless you ask. Never try to be a mind reader.

The bottom line is aside from true sociopaths, people aren't natural liars, and saying one thing while thinking something else can actually cause physical discomfort. That's what causes people to squirm. Plus there are verbal cues like *expected to, probably, basically, should be*—those qualifiers crop up when someone is trying to obscure doubts or worries.

Think

As I said before, liars try to circumvent a direct answer by referencing past answers to different questions. Phrases like: *To the best of my knowledge* are evasive maneuvers, designed to get away from telling the truth or having to tell a bald-faced lie.

Once you master the basics of detecting the smart asses from the real players, you can use that skill to grow your business.

Networking

I used to love attending networking events and crowded conferences. Being an extrovert, it always felt great networking with people of all walks of life and sizing up in a heartbeat who was real and who was a total waste of time. But then I realized that those networking events are a total waste of time. I began only attending conferences when invited as a panelist or keynote speaker. And that's when it all started to work like a charm. The key is to get the most out of your time so you can focus on what will improve your business.

Stop obsessive networking

The more people you know—really know—the more likely you are to make that important connection you need to take your career, company, or venture to the next level. All the rest is a waste of time. I am fascinated by the number of people who keep aggressively requesting to connect with me on social media and then totally vanish for years as if we never connected. Why on earth did they take so much effort to connecting with me in the first place without any follow-up—just to have me as a number on their respective profiles? What a waste of effort and time.

Once again, networking should not be about meeting as many people as possible in as short amount of time as possible. I work hard to figure out what I can do for someone else when I meet them. Who I can connect them to, what I can do for them, what resource or information I can share that will help them out. True connection is a two-way street.

Be selective

I attend one event a week. If I pick a new event, and it's not right for me, I don't go back. If it ends up being a good use of my time, where I meet quality people who are interesting and interested, then it makes it onto my list of events to attend in the future. One such event I organize on a bi-monthly basis is the Financial Policy Council events in New York City, which attracts almost 150 people every other month. There is an unspoken rule that people don't sell to each other there; it's strictly about getting to know new people and to give everyone a place to make new valuable connections. That is the key for success.

Be focused

One of my colleagues makes it a point to only meet one person at any given event and spends his time really getting to know that one person. He relies on that deep connection to potentially connect him with the rest of their network. I am not as hyper-focused, but try to have a meaningful conversation with only about five people at every event I attend or for each day of a conference. This results in enough contacts to plan one day of meetings and get to know each of them more deeply within a couple of weeks of the initial introduction. I have found that seeking to establish a quality relationship with a few people provides the greatest payoff for my efforts; you need to find what best works for you. Make the commitment to follow through or else you are wasting everyone's time.

Follow up

If someone doesn't follow-up with someone within ten days after meeting them, it was never meant to happen. That's my way of determining those who are really serious about establishing a relationship and those just connecting for the sake of connecting. You will also find that many people think that just by soliciting you at a conference they can sell you on anything they want. Then when you face them with reality, they get very frustrated because they didn't get what they were looking for and drop you as fast as they met you. Welcome to the age of shallowness and stupidity.

Keep Honing Your Skills

Becoming a successful leader does not happen by accident. It requires ongoing commitment to develop the skills that will lead to success. The single most important skill in professional and personal relationships is listening. Ernest Hemingway once said, "When people talk, listen completely. Most people never listen." It was an astute observation. Most people have their own agenda and are too busy talking—or waiting to talk—to listen to anyone else. So if you break the mold and truly listen with empathy, it will eventually help you get what you want.

Likewise, empathy is another rare trait, perhaps because it seems counterintuitive. But when you want something from someone, instead of asking for it, help that person get what they want. If you don't know what that is, simply ask how you can help them. Since so many people are out to only help themselves, when you genuinely offer to help others succeed in their goals and dreams, you'll stand out. And those people you genuinely help will in turn fight to help you succeed. Help others first without expecting, and the return will be enormous.

As important as it is to listen and help others, to get what you want, you will eventually need to tell people what that is. But nobody wants a sales pitch. So instead of trying a hard sell, focus on telling a story that captivates your audience by painting a vivid picture of your vision. When you get good at storytelling, people want to be part of that story, and they'll want to help others become part of that story too.

Part of good storytelling is passion. You don't need to be bouncing off the walls to convince someone of something. You just need to reveal your true passion, in the way that's genuine for you.

But remember; while passion is contagious, so is a lack of it. If you're not passionate about what you're talking about, why should someone else care? If you want something, you must be more excited and dedicated to it than anyone else. If you're not passionate about it, maybe it's not really that important to you, so you should consider a pivot.

Lastly, Be Accountable

The best leaders know that the buck stops with them. If you take the credit for your company's success, then be accountable for any mistakes you make. Everyone makes mistakes, and everyone knows that. It's usually not the mistake that's a problem; it's when you make a mistake and are too proud or embarrassed to be vulnerable, fess up, and apologize. Just say you're sorry so you can move on. Conversely, sincere gratitude is a powerful emotion and opens up many doors.

In general you will find that the most important tools for success aren't what college degrees you have, your accounting skills, or your engineering prowess. It's the intangibles that will set you apart the most and prepare you for the rapidly changing future. After all is said and done, it's not what you really say to people that matters most but how you make them feel. Make it a breathtaking and unforgettable event. Make it a shock and awe experience.

Chapter 13
Disruption 4.0

In times of widespread chaos and confusion, it has been the duty of more advanced human beings—artists, scientists, clowns, and philosophers—to create order. In times such as ours, however, when there is too much order, too much management, too much programming and control, it becomes the duty of superior men and women to fling their favorite monkey wrenches into the machinery. To relieve the repression of the human spirit, they must sow doubt and disruption.

—Tom Robbins

Since the start of the modern era, the so-called civilized world has experienced three industrial revolutions that disrupted the status quo and prompted economic, technological, social, and cultural evolution.

Prior to the mid-1700s, most people on Earth lived in small, rural farming communities. Life was hard and short, wages meager, and diseases rampant. Self-sufficiency was the hallmark of the time, with families growing most of their own food, sewing their own clothes, and building their own furniture using hand tools.

The first industrial revolution arrived around the 1760s and the next hundred years was noted for the emergence of machinery such as the steam engine and forging, which turned the country from an agrarian economy to one dependent on industrialization, and created a new market for coal as the fuel to power ever more powerful steam engines needed as the railroad industry grew.

At the end of the nineteenth century, the second industrial age arrived bringing innovations such as the combustible engine; new energy sources in electricity, oil, and gas; widespread use of synthetic fibers; automobiles; planes, and mass communications including the telegraph and the telephone. It can be argued that the second industrial age brought more disruption and change more quickly in more industries than any other period to date. City populations grew, factories reflected manufacturing demand, the world got smaller as the speed of news increased, traveling around the world could now be done in months, not years; and national economies were no longer isolated.

The late 1960s heralded the countercultural revolution as well as the third industrial revolution, which rode in on an electronic wave. Transistors led to microprocessors that led to personal computers and robotics. Then less than fifty years later, we are now into a new revolution.

From a business perspective where the first industrial revolution used steam to mechanize production, the second used electricity to create mass production, and the third was driven by electronics and IT, the fourth industrial revolution is all about digital technology. And entrepreneurs who want to succeed in this 4.0 world will need to understand the extent and depth of these changes and how they impact production, management, and business, financial, and other operating systems and processes. Historically, businesses have dealt in the physical world, but now there is a growing virtual world in which businesses can connect to and coordinate with employees, customers, and vendors in real-time. That same instantaneous communication has fundamentally changed how we deal with one another. Consider this: it's estimated that every sixty seconds as many as three million messages are posted on Facebook, about half a million tweets are shared, and forty million texts are sent.

Digital technology is also the basis for the Internet of things (IoT), the network of smart devices such as phones, cars, buildings, appliances, televisions, digital home assistants that are embedded with software, sensors, and network connectivity that enables these items to collect and exchange data with one another.

That crush of information is dubbed *big data*. One of the largest sources of big data is transactional data, which includes everything from stock prices to bank data to a merchant's purchase history, to supply chain operations. That amount of data being generated is so voluminous that it would be impossible to compile, sort, and analyze by hand. Only specialized software is capable of such a task. But even the most sophisticated software can only do what it's coded for, so artificial intelligence is used to correlate massive data in a useful way to identify patterns and trends.

These technological advances aren't just academic exercises. They have direct impact on business, and an entrepreneur needs to understand how to harness those benefits. One advantage a founder has compared to an established large corporation is the agility to implement new processes that produce intelligent data that can lead to improved efficiency such as in inventory tracking, customer purchase histories, infrastructure expansion, and security systems. Successful entrepreneurs in this digital age will be those who embrace disruption, can pivot quickly, and figure out how to personalize technology to best fit their needs. Think of how Uber used a mobile app to completely disrupt the taxi industry.

A January 2019 white paper by the World Economic Forum presented several case studies showing how smart factories—called lighthouses in the report—are using 4IR best practices at scale. Rather than replacing operators with machines, lighthouse factories are transforming work to make it less repetitive, better diversified, and more productive. They found that lighthouses have adapted their operations in the areas of connectivity, AI, and automation.

Klaus Schwab, founder and Executive Chairman of World Economic Forum, notes, "We stand on the brink of a technological revolution that will fundamentally alter the way we live, work, and relate to one another. In its scale, scope, and complexity, the transformation will be unlike anything humankind has experienced before. We do not yet know just how it will unfold, but one thing is clear: the response to it must be integrated and comprehensive, involving all stakeholders of the global polity, from the public and private sectors to academia and civil society."

The potential problem I foresee in both established companies and start-ups is one of stasis. Sometimes the more experience you have, the harder it is to break from conventional mindsets. Leading companies often get stuck in old business models. Microsoft executives doubted the value of online search as a revenue model. Barnes and Noble seemed convinced that people would always want a physical book in their hand. I've also made the mistake multiple times, thinking that one specific product idea would be the key to a successful business.

So instead of looking for one specific market gap, think much more big picture about what kind of market you want to be in for the long run. Research the existing players and their approaches, analyze the trends in the market related to emerging technology, then think about the timing and whether or not you can ride a disruptive wave.

But to do that you also have to be secure and critical enough to challenge the traditional ways of doing things. You'll need to buck conventional wisdom when facing new challenges and not settle for incremental thinking. You must keep learning so you can take advantage of the technological advances that seem to be happening at warp speed. Instead of viewing them as science fiction, approach them for what they are: tools. Just like CRM, Quick Books, and patents are tools for advancing productivity, AI, 3-D printing, and other disruptive technologies are just digital tools that are only as valuable as the ways they are implemented. At the same time, don't get caught up in the early adopter trap; just because it's a shiny new toy doesn't necessarily mean it will be superior in all circumstances Yes, you should design ways to test deeply held assumptions about your market but keep an open mind that different is not always better, so seek to understand the insight inherent in conventional wisdom as well as its blind spots.

A corollary to that is not shying away from healthy debate. We have this current tendency to polarize viewpoints so they are unbridgeable, when in fact there is almost always overlap if you drop your defenses enough to see it. Debate can foster insight, provided the conflict is among ideas and not among people. Instead of existing only in a bubble of like-minded peers and associates where the only sound you hear is an echo of your own views, listen carefully and approach alternative views with an open mind. Don't become a prisoner of your own myopic mental model. Full disclosure: I am still honing my skills in this regard, but I am fast learning the benefits. It is not enough to simply be comfortable with disagreement when it occurs. Critical thinkers seek out those who truly see the world differently and try hard to understand why. Often you will still disagree with these mavericks, but at times they will reframe your own thinking for the better. Never be afraid to dare and challenge anyone as long as your arguments are factual and well researched. Even if you don't ultimately accept another viewpoint or make the decision to adopt a new technology right away, at least you are aware of it and can anticipate how it will impact your business in the coming months and years.

Global Economy

The world economy is now subject to the butterfly effect; a manufacturing slowdown in Asia can have significant impacts on Main Street USA, which is why today's entrepreneurs must be informed on not just their local market but global markets as well. But which regions and countries will emerge as the main IR4 players is still open to debate in 2019. Take China. Most Chinese businessmen I know don't talk about politics, but like entrepreneurs everywhere prosperity is their goal too. But their political and social structures create different pressures. The Chinese economy is free in the sense of being market-driven, but the hand of the state is everywhere. And in my opinion, that will hold their economy back in the long run.

It was once thought that Chinese global economic supremacy was inevitable. That perception has changed among many. The double-digit growth China experienced in the three decades after it began free-market reforms in 1978 is a thing of the past. It's easy to achieve 15 percent growth when you're starting from a poor, agrarian baseline; just move peasants into the cities and let foreign investors build factories to employ them. But after that phase, boosting labor force productivity is significantly slower-going.

Since the 2008 global financial crisis, China's economic growth has been in the 6 to 8 percent range most years, and even that has been artificially maintained through massive deficit spending, mostly on infrastructure and other fixed-asset investments that don't directly contribute to future growth. As a result, its banking sector is plagued by nonperforming loans. In 2017, Moody's and the S&P downgraded China's credit rating for the first time in decades. This credit expansion will eventually have to be dialed back, reducing Chinese economic growth further.

In addition, demography will cut into future growth. The ratio of working-age to overall population in China is projected to decline precipitously, the result of the country's three-decades-long one-child policy, which was abandoned in 2015 in favor of a two-child policy. As the population ages, labor costs increase, savings go down, and healthcare costs go up, to name just a few of the growth-slowing implications.

Finally, China's future growth will be inhibited by the fact that the rest of the world has lost patience with its unfair trade practices, copyright infringements, and other transgressions that were long tolerated. More critical to businesses with parts of their supply chains China-based, the country might experience political instability as its growth slows. The predominantly urban, literate population that was willing to sacrifice its political rights in exchange for 15 percent annual growth may not be so willing to continue that trade-off when the state can only deliver 5 percent growth.

That is just one example of how geopolitical factors can be just as important to the future of today's start-ups as disruptive technologies are. How will the current EU upheaval shake out? Will Africa emerge as a fertile ground for a new generation of unicorns? What opportunities will there be in India? Will social upheaval in South America impact mining that produces the industrial metals digital technology relies on? There will always be questions like this; no entrepreneurs will have all the answers, but just having a greater degree of awareness of what is going on in different parts of the globe and taking that into your calculus will put you ahead of the game.

You Cannot Stop Technology

There was a time when the horseless carriage was seen as an indulgence for the wealthy. Television was viewed as a novelty. Computers were a lab tool for academia. AI the stuff of scary science fiction. By nature most humans resist change because it moves them out of their comfort zones. Entrepreneurs are people, and they are equally prone to the same resistance, especially because it may not seem to make financial sense in the beginning. Almost all exponential technologies needed time to find their sweet spots. Then once they do, it quickly becomes mainstream, blockchain being just the most recent example. Companies are already implementing blockchain as a way to keep better track of supply chain specifics. In five years it's likely start-ups not employing blockchain technologies will likely be at a disadvantage.

Software as a Service (SaaS) will also continue to disrupt most traditional industries. Uber is just a software app; the company doesn't own any cars but is now the biggest taxi company in the world. Airbnb does not own any properties but is now the biggest hotel company in the world. The next disruptive start-up is just an idea away.

As with any revolution, there is a domino or ripple effect, creating problems creative entrepreneurs will solve.

The Ripple Effect

Sometime in the 2020s self-driving vehicles will be on the market, disrupting many industries and creating others.

You won't need to own a car any more; you'll order an autonomous electric car that will drive you to your destination.

While en route you'll be able to return email or make phone calls, improving productivity. Once you reach your destination, there'll be no reason to park, so the need for parking lots will diminish, and those spaces can be replaced by parks.

Autonomous cars will be safer because a main cause of accidents—driver distraction—will no longer be an issue. Fewer accidents means saving many of the 1.2 million people who currently die each year in car accidents worldwide.

With profits plummeting, traditional car companies try the evolutionary approach and just build a better car, while tech companies (Tesla, Apple, Google) will do the revolutionary approach and build a computer on wheels. Electric cars will become mainstream, making cities less noisy and polluted.

Insurance companies will have massive trouble because without accidents the current car insurance model becomes unworkable. Who will come up with its replacement?

Disruptive technology is always a double-edged blade. On one hand, it will make certain jobs obsolete, but inevitably it creates new careers and business opportunities for those who look around corners. If you think of a niche you want to go in, ask yourself: *In the future, is it likely this niche will exist?* If the answer is yes, figure out how can you make that happen sooner. Hypothetically it's reasonable for you to assume that any idea designed for success in the twentieth century is eventually doomed to fail in the twenty-first century.

Welcome to the fourth Industrial Revolution. Welcome to the Exponential Age.

But …

Some things won't change. While technologies and related best practices evolve, the fundamentals of business discussed in previous chapters will remain as important as ever. In the next section are some case studies and examples of spectacular failures, implosions, and self-destruction. These are cautionary tales of what happens when you ignore sound business fundamentals, regardless of how cutting edge your product or service may be.

PART III

LESSONS FROM REAL-LIFE FAILURES AND CAUTIONARY TALES

While it is very true that you learn more from failure than you do from success; you can save yourself time, money, and tears by learning from other people's mistakes to avoid start-up saboteurs such as suspect systems and strategies, money mismanagement, lackluster leadership, market miscues, and other fatal flaws that can inhibit growth, drain cash flow, and ultimately doom your business.

The first five chapters in this final section present brief post mortems of high-profile flameouts; cautionary tales that provide crucial lessons learned that will benefit both novice and experienced entrepreneurs alike.

The final two chapters address the dark side of venture capital and Silicon Valley, which may be the biggest start-up saboteurs of them all.

Chapter 14
Pets.com

Founded: 1998; **Failed**: 2000

Background

On November 21, 1994, the Pets.com domain name was registered by a Pasadena, California, entrepreneur named Greg McLemore, who that same year founded WebMagic.com. as an online incubator, looking to cash in on buying domain names. His portfolio of sites included cooking.com and entrepreneurs.com. And McLemore did enjoy some early Internet era success registering the toys.com domain name and starting an online toy store that was eventually sold to eToys in 1998.

Around that same time McLemore was contacted by Harvard Business School student Carolyn Everson who wanted to buy the pets. com domain name to found an online pet store start-up. McLemore didn't want to sell but agreed to partner with Everson, eager to tap into the multi-billion dollar pet products industry. Both McLemore and Everson believed their business model would be a slam dunk. They assumed pet owners would want to buy pet food and accessories online, even though in 1998 the Internet was still a new technology using dial-up connections, e-commerce was a fledgling platform, and nobody knew for sure how consumers would feel about buying anything sight unseen from cyberspace instead of at a physical store where they could see and touch products.

The partners secured VC money from Hummer Winblad and launched pets.com in November 1998, and the company was incorporated the following February. They hired Julie Wainwright as CEO. In a 2014 interview, she said, "I said the only way I would join Pets.com was if I could get Amazon to invest and I did. I knew that anything that could be sourced externally, Amazon could do better and cheaper than anyone else."

Amazon, which Jeff Bezos had founded a few years earlier in 1995, invested some cash in exchange for 50 percent ownership. Bezos's interest makes sense; pet.com was to pets what Amazon was to books.

But Pets.com would move forward without one of its founders. Carolyne Everson would later reveal her vision for the company did not match Wainwright's.

"We met and disagreed about the business," she said at an entrepreneur event at Montclair State University in April 2019. When Everson got home from their meeting, she received a fax stating that her services were no longer required.

Flush with VC cash, Amazon support, and a distinctive sock puppet "spokesperson," Wainwright launched a massive marketing campaign, which started with a commercial during the 2000 Superbowl, costing $1.2 million, followed by an online, print, TV, and radio blitz. That November the Pets.com sock puppet appeared in the Macy's Thanksgiving

Parade. There was no doubt they had achieved brand awareness, and consumers began to order pet supplies and accessories from the site. So the business went public and raised more than $80 million dollars in its IPO. Life was good. Unfortunately the business model wasn't.

Demand was falling significantly short of expectations. All that awareness wasn't translating to comparable online sales. Perhaps if anyone had thought to do a deep dive into the market, they might have realized that in 2000 there was a problem with the consumer value proposition. The lack of expected revenue created a cash crunch because the company had spent a lot of money securing huge warehouses to store the products they anticipated selling.

In an effort to jumpstart sales, Pets.com started offering discounted and at times free delivery, a costly proposition considering how much big bags of dog food weigh. The gambit did improve sales but ate up the profit—and then some—per transaction. It was an unsustainable model, and in November 2000 Pets.com closed.

At the time Wainwright said: "It is well known that this is a very, very difficult environment for business-to-consumer Internet companies. With no better offers and avenues effectively exhausted, we felt that the best option was an orderly wind-down with the objective to try to return something back to the shareholders."

In 2014 she told sfgate.com, "We needed $285 million just to break even. That's the cost of getting a business to scale. And we were already early stage. We couldn't get the second round of financing from the stock market, and we had to shut down."

Yes, in today's market online pet stores thrive, so you might want to say Pets.com was ahead of its time, which is simply a polite way of saying they were out of step with their current marketplace. Whatever the perspective, Pets.com burned through $300 million in less than two years. It is still widely considered by many as the biggest dotcom flop in American Internet history.

Cause of Death

Product development failure due to lack of market research.

Lesson Learned

You must target an existing market, not hope to create a market. There is a good reason the majority of successful products are developed after a thorough market analysis that would identify current consumer need and desire.

Postmortem

Carolyn Everson went on to become VP of Global Marketing Solutions at Facebook.

"When I had to really abandon the dream of starting Pets.com, I have to be honest and tell you those first couple of weeks were devastating. I was really, really down and I wasn't quite sure what to do next. And then I realized that I am just graduating from B-school, I have great experience, I'm going to be an asset to another company. I had to get my feet back on the ground and get my confidence back."

Julie Wainwright is CEO and founder of the RealReal, a luxury e-commerce consignment boutique.

"You cannot be afraid of failure–that fear will prevent you from taking risks required to move forward. The media didn't hold back when it came to Pets.com failing; however, failing so publicly freed me from worrying about failing again–it pushed me to take greater risks, and it forced me to think outside of myself. Part of that was realizing that if I wanted to have my dream job, I would have to create it, and that's what I did with the RealReal."

Pets.com: PetSmart bought the Pets.com domain name in December 2000 for an undisclosed amount.

Chapter 15
Boo.com

Born: 1998; **Failed**: May 2000

Background

Boo.com was a UK dotcom created to sell branded fashion apparel over the Internet to fashion-forward customers. The company was founded in 1998 by Ernst Malmsten and Kajsa Leander. They envisioned a lifestyle destination site where a pixilated fashionista sales assistant, named Ms. Boo, would assist shoppers find clothes that matched their personalities and style sense.

Malmsten and Leander had first met as young children while attending the same nursery school in Sweden, then again as teenagers going to the same high school. Their paths crossed again when they ran into each other at a Paris nightclub as young adults, both facing professional crossroads—him as a poetry critic, her as a former *Vogue* model. They collaborated on creating an online bookstore, Bokus. com, which in 1997 became the third-largest bookseller in 1997. They sold Bokus for a profit, and that success inspired a move to London and founding boo.com in 1998 along with fellow Swede Patrik Hedelin.

Thanks to Bokus.com Malmsten and Leander were considered successful and sophisticated Internet entrepreneurs in the eyes of European investors. So when their business plan called for £20 million in start-up funds, thirty employees, and three months to launch, nobody questioned their ambition. But by the time boo.com launched in October 1999, the start-up employed about four hundred staff in eight offices and had burned through multiples of that original cost estimate.

The problems were legion. First were the technical issues. Boo.com relied heavily on JavaScript and Flash technology. That's status quo today, but in the late 1990s most households were still using dial-up, so would-be customers had to wait several minutes for the page to load. More problematic was that their business model had not anticipated issues any global company would face, such as the need to function in different languages, and having country-specific pricing and tax structures for the eighteen countries they sold in.

But the partners were undaunted—faltering business plan be damned—because before boo.com had gone live online, *Fortune* magazine had dubbed it one of Europe's trendiest companies. While the darling of the business and investment set, their branding had failed to reach the masses. As the business struggled to get sales, research indicated only about 13 percent of Internet users were aware of the name; for non-Internet users that brand awareness fell to a minuscule 1.4 percent.

According to reports at the time, boo.com spent £83 million (USD $135 million) in just six months to market itself as a global company.

Not only weren't their sales as brisk as expected, they were beset with more product returns than anticipated.

According to reports at the time, boo.com spent £83 million (USD $135 million) in just six months to market itself as a global company. Not only weren't their sales as brisk as expected, they were beset with more returns than anticipated. And since boo.com's founders had decided to pay postage for returns, it exacerbated the financial bloodletting.

Over April and May of 2000, boo.com made £200,000 and had 300,000 visitors. The start-up sought $30 million from American investors to stay afloat, but by then the Nasdaq had already started its freefall. The dotcom bubble was officially starting to burst, and no bank would lend them more money. So boo.com became the UK's first high-profile Internet collapse, leaving investors that included JP Morgan, Goldman Sachs, Bernard Arnault, and the Benetton family holding an empty bag. Boo.com's four hundred-plus employees and contractors were left unpaid.

Liquidators KPMG were summoned on May 17, 2000.

Soon after, Malmsten and Leander wrote a book, *Boo Hoo: A Dotcom Story* (Random House, 2001) detailing their perspective of the debacle. Famous Malmsten quoted from the book: "After the pampered luxury of a Lear jet 35, Concorde was a bit cramped."

A few years later Malmsten told the *Guardian*, "We were too soon and trying to do too much, but those were the times."

Cause of Death

Overly ambitious goals, launching in multiple European countries simultaneously without necessary infrastructure.

Lesson Learned

Starting a business without a well-thought-out, realistic, highly-detailed business plan that factors in all aspects of rollout is a recipe for disaster.

Postmortem

Ernst Malmsten started a consulting business, RedGreenZebra Creative Management in 2003 and was named CEO in 2011 for London-based luxury goods company Lara Bohinc.

Kajsa Leander founded Berga Bruk in 2015, which makes "innovative beverages from organic Swedish apples and berries."

Boo.com's domain was bought by US-based online retailer Fashionmall.com and relaunched. The proprietary technology developed for boo.com sold for £250,000.

Chapter 16

Wesabe

Born: 2006; **Failed**: 2010

Background

Wesabe was founded by Marc Hedlund and his high school buddy Jason Knight to help people manage their personal finances by using a Web 2.0 approach. At the time, online finance start-ups were part of the Internet zeitgeist, so Hedlund and Knight knew there was competition all around them. But Wesabe had the buzz and was considered the leader in online personal finance race. Until Mint came along ten months later and eventually ran Wesabe off the Internet.

The main reason for that was Hedlund's methodical—a nice way of saying plodding—approach that he took after choosing not to work with Yodlee, which provided automatic financial data aggregation as a Web service. Hedlund later said he felt Yodlee was "crumbling, having failed to get acquired and losing executives. They were also very aggressive in negotiation, telling us they would give us six months' service nearly free and then tell us the final price we'd be charged going forward."

Instead, Hedlund decided to create his own proprietary data acquisition system technology, but displayed no apparent sense of urgency and took far too long to build it, allowing Mint to catch up and eventually pass Wesabe.

While taking too long to build their proprietary software doomed Wesabe, the nail in the coffin was an error of focus. As Hedlund explains: "I prioritized trying to build tools that would eventually help people change their financial behavior for the better, which I believed required people to more closely work with and understand their data. I was focused on trying to make the usability of editing data as easy and functional as it could be. Mint focused on making the user do almost no work at all, by automatically editing and categorizing their data, reducing the number of fields in their signup form, and giving them immediate gratification as soon as they possibly could. Their approach completely kicked our approach's ass."

In a blog he wrote not long after Wesabe failed, Hedlund noted: "You can't blame your competitors or your board or the lack of or excess of investment. Focus on what really matters: making users happy with your product as quickly as you can.... If you do those better than anyone else out there you'll win."

Cause of Death

Time mismanagement. Decided to create proprietary software in-house rather than paying another company. The process took so long that it allowed a competitor to gain a foothold and eventually pass Wesabe by.

Lesson Learned

Time matters; if you cannot do everything on your own, stick to your strengths, outsource the rest, and focus on customers' ease of doing business.

Postmortem

Marc Hedlund has held numerous positions in the online industry and became senior director of engineering at MailChimp in 2017.

Chapter 17
Juicero

Born: 2013; **Failed**: Sept. 2017

Background

The fact the Juicero's founder compared himself to Steve Jobs should have been the first red flag.

In 2013 Doug Evans came up with an idea for a Wi-Fi-connected juicer that would use proprietary, single-serving packets of pre-juiced fruits and vegetables provided to consumers via subscription. He referred to it as the Tesla of juicers. (Red flag #2) He founded the start-up Juicero and by only presenting 3D-printed renderings of the pitched product raised $120 million in Silicon Valley venture capital, including money from Kleiner Perkins Caufield & Byers, Alphabet Inc., and the Campbell Soup Company.

Evans boasted that his juicing device exerted 8,000 pounds of pressure to cold-press the freshest juice possible from produce packs that provided information about the farm of origin and the date of harvest, which would never exceed five days. Unpasteurized, organic, fresh juice was just a Juicero squeeze away.

When promoting his device, Evans commented: "I have a belief that everything you put in your mouth is a life or death decision."

Perhaps not for the consumer, but it eventually was for his company and its high-priced juicer that initially listed at $700 (later reduced to $400). It didn't take long for consumers—and investors—to realize the device was superfluous. In April 2017 Bloomberg News reported that the juice bags, which cost $5 to $7 each, could be hand-squeezed and produce just as much juice just as fast—and in some cases faster—than by using the expensive Juicero cold-press machine.

Juicero went into immediate spin mode, but the damage was irreversible. In September 2017, the company suspended sale of the machines and produce packs and released a statement that announced: "Creating an effective manufacturing and distribution system for a nationwide customer base requires infrastructure that we cannot achieve on our own as a standalone business." The release also reported Juicero was searching for a buyer "with an existing national fresh food supply chain," and it offered consumers a refund for the following ninety days.

In a 2018 interview with *Vice News Tonight*, Evans was asked what the media got wrong about Juicero.

"Everything. They got stuck on a narrative. It's not even worth my breath. I'm done."

That he was.

Since then Juicero has since become Exhibit A in how Silicon Valley VCs have an increasing tendency to raise ginormous amounts of money to create solutions to non-problems.

Cause of Death
Self-inflicted wound.

Lesson Learned
No amount of VC money or good marketing can save a bad product. Period.

Postmortem
Doug Evans's pursuit after Juicero was promoting the alleged benefits of "raw" water—unfiltered, untreated, unsterilized water collected from natural springs that sells for $15 or more per jug. (Doctors warn that untreated water carries potential health risks such as pathogens and dangerous chemicals, so buyer beware.)

Chapter 18
Pay by Touch

Born: 2002; **Failed**: May 2008

Background

Pay by Touch was the brainchild of John Rogers, who managed to raise $340 million in venture capital for a high-tech start-up looking to implementing biometric authentication technology that would transform how Americans paid for goods and services—with a thumbprint rather than a credit card or cash. The technology would also provide secure access to checking, credit card, loyalty, healthcare, and personal information.

It was am ambitious idea, with biometrics requiring both advanced hardware and software—meaning it would also be an enterprise requiring significant investment. Rogers's investors included the Gordon

P. Getty Family Trust and the Silicon Valley-based Mobius Venture Capital ($37 million), the OZ Master Fund of New York's Och-Ziff Capital Management ($62 million); Connecticut-based Plainfield Asset Management ($67.5 million); and Denarius Touch, a unit of Thomas Steyer's San Francisco-based Farallon Capital Management, ($45.1 million) as well as numerous wealthy individuals.

Apparently, before handing over millions to him, none of his VC or private investors had thought to do a thorough background check. If they had, they would have discovered some troubling information. Prior to moving to San Francisco, Rogers had lived in Minneapolis where he socialized with lawyers and stockbrokers and eventually convinced them to invest in a chain of chiropractic clinics. He told investors he had a pool of personal injury attorneys who would refer clients to the clinics. But the clinics failed and several creditors, including one of the chiropractors he employed sued for unpaid wages. They never collected.

His legal problems extended beyond financial matters. He had been arrested three times: once for allegedly abusing a former girlfriend, another time for allegedly trashing a different girlfriend's house after she filed a restraining order against him, and lastly on a narcotics violation after a policeman claimed to see him using cocaine while driving. A former landlady sued Rogers in 2001 for skipping out on his rent. Eventually Rogers left Minneapolis and headed west to the welcoming arms of Silicon Valley.

Pay by Touch faced many challenges beyond developing the technology such as migrating consumers to ACH from pin and signature-based transactions and over time, growing rumors of John Roger's reputation as a free-spending, hard-partying, drug-using bon vivant. More troubling to investors were his business decisions.

According to an sfgate.com report, Pay by Touch "spent more than $150 million buying out rival firms that also were pursuing biometric bill-paying, court records show. Pay by Touch also went on a hiring spree: at one point, more than 750 people worked there. Rogers also leased 90,000 square feet of prime office space in a new Mission Street high-rise. The company made some sales, signing contracts with the Albertson's and Piggly Wiggly supermarket chains to install payment terminals. But the company never came close to breaking even. In 2007, Pay By Touch lost $137 million on $600,000 in revenues." By May of 2007 the company was unable to meet payroll.

When Rogers found out fellow executives were promoting a change of leadership, Rogers lashed out, sending threatening emails to company employees as well as investors, which prompted talks of an attempted intervention.

As Pay by Touch started running into troubles, Rogers's lifestyle—and how that may have negatively impacted his business decisions—came under increasing scrutiny and his history eventually came to light. After Pay by Touch filed for bankruptcy in 2007, Rogers was accused of domestic abuse, drug possession, and misuse of investor money, but no criminal charges were ever brought.

Cause of Death
Extravagance

Lesson Learned
Character counts. A lot. The right leadership can be more important than the right idea, the right team, or even the right business model. Smart investors do proper diligence. If you are a fake entrepreneur, you'll be found out eventually.

Postmortem
John Rogers. According to LinkedIn, the former founder of Solidus Networks (Pay by Touch's corporate arm) is now chairman for Odysseus Global Technology and founder of Odysseus Trust.

Chapter 19

The Rise of the Unicorns and the Loss of Rational Thinking

Sometimes we all need a unicorn to believe in. Sometimes we need a unicorn to believe in us.

—Claudia Bakker

In the investment industry, a unicorn is defined as a privately-held tech company started since 2003 with a valuation of US$1 billion or more. This is the holy grail every VC seeks, the next Uber, the next Slack, the next Airbnb. VCs will pour tens and hundreds of millions of dollars into such companies in the crossed-fingers hope they will one day turn into the next Microsoft, Apple, or Amazon.

The chances are slim. According to *Entrepreneur* magazine, a typical VC meets with one thousand new companies a year and funds two of them. For every 10,000 start-ups that get funding, only one becomes a unicorn. Do the math and the chances of a VC finding its unicorn work out to about one in five million. And it's not a fast process even if you win the start-up lottery. According to data compiled by Visual Capitalist, it takes an average of six years for a start-up to go from founding to unicorn, an incubation that has remained constant since 2003. That means years of funneling massive amounts of cash into (hopefully) the next Big Thing.

Perhaps no cautionary tale reflects the hubris of Silicon Valley's unicorn pursuit more than the debacle of Theranos and its founder Elizabeth Holmes, who conned the crème de la VC crème with her claim to have found not just a disruptive technology for blood testing, but a method that would transform medicine itself. Rarely has the pursuit of the unicorn fostered such a lack of basic business checks and balances like, oh, I don't know… maybe asking to actually see the device work in front of your own eyes and not just taking someone's word for it. Or taking a moment to contemplate how a college dropout without so much as a biology degree could devise a portable device touted to replace proven blood testing technology and do it all with a single drop of blood gotten by a painless finger prick rather than a drawing blood with a needle and syringe.

Yes, college dropout computer geeks are known for coming up with amazing technology that has disrupted many industries. But medicine is different. If for no other reason than it's people's actual lives we're talking about. When it came to Theranos, the pursuit of the next unicorn turned into a folie à deux, the madness fueled by a loss of rational thinking by VCs who chose selective vision over best practices and Holmes's unbridled craving for fame, inclusion, and respect. Instead of a world-changing breakthrough, what the VCs got was a Silicon Valley *Game of Thrones*.

As a kid growing up in Washington, DC, Holmes dreamed of being a doctor, like her great-great-grandfather. But a phobia of needles put the kibosh on that career path. So after getting accepted at Stanford, she studied chemical engineering. But she wasn't fully focused on her studies. Another childhood dream—to be a billionaire—was driving her to found her own start-up, which she later said was a tool for making a change in the world.

Her first idea was for a skin patch that would test for infectious diseases in the blood and then deliver antibiotics to treat the illness. When she told one of her professors about it, their reaction was blunt; they said laudable but ludicrous. Holmes's response was to apply for a patent on it and to go ask another professor, Channing Robertson, to go into business with her. He agreed.

She dropped out of Stanford the following semester in 2003 and founded Real-Time Cures, which later became Theranos. Her product idea changes as well to a device that could run any diagnostic test with just a drop or two of blood on a machine she called the Edison. Holmes's pitch was that the tests would be able to detect everything from cancer to high cholesterol and everything in between. By December 2004, Holmes had raised $6 million from the likes of Oracle founder Larry Ellison and venture capitalist Tim Draper who founded Draper Fisher Jurvetson (and who happened to be a childhood friend's father.) And she got her investors to agree that she did not have to reveal to them how the technology worked. And she would have final say over every decision having to do with the company. In other words they agreed to absolutely no checks or balances.

What could possibly go wrong? Well, everything, it turns out.

In 2005 Theranos hired British scientist Ian Gibbons to develop the technology Holmes was promising. We know now that it didn't take Gibbons long to realize her world-changing idea simply was not feasible at this time. But he still spent years trying to come up with *something*.

And during all that time people kept raining money on Theranos and touting Holmes as a wunderkind. She was on the cover of *Fortune* and *Forbes*, was invited to TED Talk, and appeared on panels with political and technological heavyweights like Alibaba's Jack Ma.

In 2010 with either narcissistic arrogance or complete delusion, Holmes entered a partnership with Walgreens based solely on her word the technology worked. It didn't. Realizing that real people were about to trust their health on a bogus technology weighed on Gibbons. But blowing the whistle would come with a cost. At the time he was fighting cancer and didn't want to lose his job or put all the Theranos employees at risk. Then in May 2013, suspecting he was about to get fired, Gibbons took an overdose of Tylenol and died a week later. Holmes kept on attracting followers and raising money—more than $700 million all told.

In April 2015 *Time* named Holmes one of the most influential people in the world. A month later *Forbes* named Holmes the youngest self-made, female billionaire in the United States. Theranos had been given a $9 billion valuation, and Holmes's stakes made her (on paper) worth $4.5 billion. That same year AZBio named Theranos 2015's Bioscience Company of the Year.

The beginning of the end occurred in the summer of 2015 when the FDA began investigating Theranos and regulators found major inaccuracies in the testing Theranos was doing on patients. Then in October a *Wall Street Journal* reporter named John Carreyrou published an exposé that Theranos was a start-up house of cards because Edison didn't work. He reported Holmes would invite potential investors to the company, take some blood, take them to lunch, then present them with the results. Except the analysis wasn't from Edison, which had proven highly unreliable. Instead Theranos techs were running the blood on standard industry machines. His information came from a whistleblower. The upshot was obvious: Holmes had crossed the line from hype to criminal fraud. It would later be revealed both the government investigations and the *WSJ* article were initiated by the same whistleblower.

Rather than do a mea culpa, Holmes doubled down. Not long after the first *WSJ* article, she appeared at a medical conference to introduce Theranos's new product, a portable minilab capable of carrying out a variety of tests, even one detecting the then-new Zika virus. Holmes claimed the device had Internet connectivity to send and verify test results.

Eventually Theranos was forced to correct and void tens of thousands of blood tests given at pharmacies where its equipment was used in 2014 and 2015.

In March 2018 Holmes and her former company president Sunny Balwani were charged with massive fraud by the Securities and Exchange Commission for "raising more than $700 million from investors through an elaborate, years-long fraud in which they exaggerated or made false statements about the company's technology, business, and financial performance." Holmes agreed to give up financial and voting control of the company, pay a $500,000 fine, and return 18.9 million shares of Theranos stock. She isn't allowed to be the director or officer of a publicly-traded company for ten years.

In June 2018, Theranos announced that Holmes was stepping down as CEO. On the same day, the Department of Justice announced that a federal grand jury had charged Holmes, along with Balwani, with nine counts of wire fraud and two counts of conspiracy to commit wire fraud. Each of them could face up to 20 years in prison, and a $250,000 fine plus restitution for each charge, the government has said.

In September 2018, Theranos sent an email to shareholders announcing it was shutting down.

I find it stunning that even after all that, some VCs defended Holmes. Then again of course they did because the scam revealed the Silicon

Valley emperors were wearing no clothes. She had no greater cheerleader than Tim Draper, who gave a delusional May 2018 interview to CNBC after the federal charges came down. His self-serving comments included: "We have taken down another great icon … She got bullied into submission … She created an incredible opportunity. It was a great vision; it was a great technology … Why is it worthless? It's worthless because this writer was like a badger going after her, like a hyena going after her, and then it became a bigger and bigger thing."

In June he appeared on Cheddar and continued defending the indefensible, claiming Holmes could have succeeded had she not been attacked and forced to fail. He also suggested the only reason Holmes was indicted was because the media "created such a strong frenzy. [Carreyrou] guy made a lot of money off of this." Draper also referred to Holmes as an icon.

Days after Holmes stepped down as CEO, his firm wrote off their Theranos investment, which was $500,000. Other investors who lost big were the Walton family ($150 million), Rupert Murdoch ($125 million), and Education Secretary Betsy DeVos ($100 million).

Draper added, "I make my money on a few extraordinary companies. Theranos was one of those extraordinary companies that could've been one of those big, huge winners."

And alchemists would have been rich had they succeeded turning lead to gold, which was also laudable but equally ludicrous. The point Draper seems to completely miss—or refuse to acknowledge—isn't that a start-up failed or that Holmes's reach exceeded her grasp. It's that he and everyone else were duped. Regardless of her initial intent, she became a con and got away with it for as long as she did because he and the others were blinded by their pursuit of a unicorn.

In the *LA Times* Mary McNamara noted: "*If it had worked out, it would have been revolutionary* is the still-delusional mantra of many who promoted or were involved in Theranos, as if somehow there had been a chance of it working out. Instead of acting as if Holmes were some freak of nature, we should be looking at the system that produced her. A system in which money, power, and prestige are given to people just because they give good meeting or have the right connections. A system that anoints people as game-changers before they've changed anything but their social status."

New York Times columnist Roger Cohen added: "Myth and manipulation turned Holmes into a billionaire. She incarnated America's collective hallucination and corruption, its vertiginous loss of bearings."

Draper might want to label the media as conspiracists who took down an "icon" but their assessment is right on target. As are those of us who understand the dangers of a business model that values growth more than profitability. Unicorns pursue market share rather than profit, so your value can be $1 billion or more without ever being in the black. But eventually somebody needs to care about the bottom line. Also, another danger of this obsession with unicorns by VCs is that it can kill innovation.

Not all VCs are big game unicorn hunters. Many, especially outside of Silicon Valley, invest in companies with much more modest valuations, understanding the home run hitters rarely win the batting title. Those VCs create wealth for both its investors and the start-up entrepreneurs and their teams.

VC Bill Gurley, a general partner at Benchmark, offers this warning: "The pressures of lofty paper valuations, massive burn rates (\and the subsequent need for more cash, and unprecedented low levels of IPOs and M&A, have created a complex and unique circumstance which many unicorn CEOs and investors are ill-prepared to navigate. In 1999, record valuations coexisted with record IPOs and shareholder liquidity. 2015 was the exact opposite. Record private unicorn valuations were offset by increasingly fewer and fewer IPOs. Everyone was successful on paper, but in terms of real cash-on-cash returns, there was little to show."

He argues that start-ups should focus on profitability to eliminate the need for a funding round. "The healthiest thing that could possibly happen is a dramatic increase in the real cost of capital and a return to an appreciation for sound business execution."

Others are also seeing the problems with a unicorn-based culture. Michael Eisenberg, who co-founded the VC Aleph in Tel Aviv, notes, "The pursuit of the unicorn status is cheapening entrepreneurship. It is also creating bizarre funding rounds where the target is a $1 billion valuation so you can be called a unicorn and then later vaporized by quixotic preference structures in a *calcified cap table*. More troubling is that the attempt to become a unicorn confuses the goal with the potential outcome."

Eisenberg says the fixation on unicorns is ripping the soul out of entrepreneurship. "The billion-dollar unicorn club is fast becoming the object of the pursuit and not the outcome of passionate innovation. This is doubly troubling. First, no great companies are born trying to become billion-dollar companies. Great companies are born from passion and desire to fix the world and not from financial pursuit."

That sounds perfectly logical, but they are the exception that proves the current rule because in Silicon Valley it primarily remains all about the unicorn, which is why widespread rational thought is so scarce. And the irony is that most VCs don't recognize a unicorn even if it hits them in the face. Frankly, VCs at large are so overestimated to the point of the ridiculous.

And whether the lessons that should have been learned from Theranos actually sink in remain to be seen although I doubt it will take long to get an answer. In March 2019 business news sites announced that former Enron chief executive Jeffrey Skilling is actively pursuing a new energy start-up, going from prison stripes to pinstripes in record time. The central figure in arguably the biggest corporate business scandal this side of Theranos, who was convicted of felony fraud and other crimes that led to Enron's collapse and sentenced to twenty-four years in prison, Skilling is reportedly holding meetings with former Enron executives seeking investors for his venture, described in some reports as a digital platform that connects investors to oil and gas projects. As of mid-2019 no VC had jumped on board yet. But the year was young.

As business journalist, Emily Sheffield, wrote in the *Evening Standard*: "In the meantime, change is still slow. Men still dominate Silicon Valley; big money will charge bloodthirstily after those tech unicorns, dazzled by the promise of a Brobdingnagian win, while serious checks and balances will be ignored."

At times it's as if the Silicon Valley inmates are running the VC asylum. But what might seem like unicorn-crazed chaos from the outside looking in is actually carefully structured. And as the next chapter shows, there's another analogy that is much more apt than most people realize.

Chapter 20
The Silicon Valley Cabal

The problem with most smart people is that they are too dumb to distinguish necessity from luxury, that's why despite having the resources to deal with real problems that cause misery to humanity, they keep wasting those resources on pompous dreams. And you can have first-hand experience with such stupidity if you visit any Silicon Valley event. Whether it is smart toilet or smart underwear, there is no end to intellectual, wealthy, and pompous stupidity. Silicon Valley is no longer the valley of innovators who solve problems; it has turned into the valley of resourceful stupidity. They are a bunch of people wasting resources on creating products that do nothing more than fuel the predominant neurosis of consumerism.

—Abhijit Naskar

One of the great trends we've been witnessing since 2010 has been what you might call the democratization of entrepreneurship. It's a powerful trend, and one that I think will have a huge impact not just on the American economy and workforce, but perhaps even more intensely on other areas of the world, particularly developing economies. Entrepreneurs don't care about pedigree. Entrepreneurial communities are networks, not hierarchies. Openness, the free flow of information, the lack of community gatekeepers, and entrepreneurs as leaders are hallmarks of these networks. As a result, the fundamental tenants that underpin these networks there is a decreased emphasis on pedigree, background, and connections. In many places entrepreneurs are rightly judged by the strength of their ideas, the value they bring to the community, and the success of their past efforts, not on their family name or where they attended school.

I fundamentally believe the world does and will further benefit from the democratization of entrepreneurship as more people look to themselves as the engine to grow beyond their circumstances. And this phrase works in reverse as well; entrepreneurship promotes democratization. Entrepreneurs value the stable systems that democracy tends to bring, they see themselves and not government as the answer to their societies challenges, they provide jobs and economic stability that promote stable society, and they work in networks that by their nature are fundamentally more democratic than hierarchical regimes.

That's how it should work. Then there's the Silicon Valley with its cabal of VC mafioso. A few years ago *Newsweek* observed: "Though Silicon Valley's newest billionaires may anoint themselves the saints of American capitalism, they're beginning to resemble something else entirely: robber barons. Behind the hoodies and flip-flops lurk businesspeople as rapacious as the black-suited and top-hatted industrialists of the late-19th century. Like their predecessors in railroads, steel, banking, and oil a century ago, Silicon Valley's new entrepreneurs are harnessing technology to make the world more efficient." Obviously, this is a good thing. But as *Newsweek* noted: "Along the way that process is bringing great economic and labor dislocation, as well as an unequal share of the spoils."

That's because like a crime syndicate, Silicon Valley's business model was really only intended for a select group, founded to commercialize mature technologies for specific markets. As *Digital Tonto* noted: "We're now entering a new era of innovation, and that model doesn't quite fit as well as it once did. We need to develop a new innovation ecosystem to stay competitive in the twenty-first century."

Back in the late 1960s, as the Cultural Revolution roiled the United States, investor Arthur Rock funded some entrepreneurs who left Fairchild Semiconductor to start their own company, which became Intel. That became the blueprint. Up to then when an entrepreneur, say in Chicago or Miami had an idea, they typically got a small business bank loan. But in the San Francisco area, entrepreneurs got funding from engineers-turned-small venture capitalists. Part of this was driven by a lack of regional industry, so the tech world was small and close-knit.

Then, according to *Digital Tonto*, "The early success of the model led to a process that was somewhat self-perpetuating. Engineers became entrepreneurs and got rich. They, in turn, became investors in new enterprises, which attracted more engineers to the region, many of whom became entrepreneurs."

Today it remains an incestuous group that seeks to keep their funding in the family; outsiders need not apply. But they are in capital denial. Animals—and even insects—avoid incest, knowing innately that it can eventually lead to deformity and possible extinction, a lesson that Silicon Valley VCs not only blithely ignore but wear like a badge of honor.

In March 2019 the *New York Times* reported: "It's part of Silicon Valley's often-incestuous circle of life. The start-up world projects a meritocratic image, but in reality, it is a small, tight-knit club where success typically hinges on whom you know. In this model, employees of tech start-ups frequently leave the companies once they have been enriched by their firms' initial public offerings. Then networks of alumni from these companies—called mafias—support their peers' new businesses with hiring, advice, and money."

For example, Airbnb's former head of data science, Riley Newman, established Wave Capital in 2017 to invest in Airbnb employees who left the company to become founders of their own start-ups. As of spring 2019, the VC is patiently waiting for Airbnb to go public so it can cash in on the wave of freshly-made millionaires to come a-calling for money to fund their own entrepreneurial dreams.

PayPal had its own mafia led by Peter Thiel and Elon Musk. Uber and the others will have their "families" as well. One obvious problem is that within their too-cozy groups, there's a tendency to be lax on the processes most mortal entrepreneurs have to go through when seeking funding. In February 2018 two long-tenured Airbnb employees set out to start their own company. Did they slave over creating a detailed prospectus, financial statements, and other fundamental advance work? Seems not. But they secured $2 million for a philanthropic start-up that seemed vividly short on specifics beyond it would facilitate people donating to charity.

Newman from Wave Capital, one of the investors, shrugged off the process, telling the *New York Times*, "These are people we know can build great products. They know us, they trust us. We know them; we trust them."

Obviously such VC-entrepreneur incest succeeds enough to perpetuate the practice, but it's also lazy and short-sighted. Wealth creation should not be just for those already wealthy or IPO millionaires looking to become billionaires. It should be available for anyone with a great idea, the willingness to work endless hours to build a company, and the savvy to do it well.

But according to a report in *Time*, "Today most of the investments in the hottest tech start-ups are happening behind the velvet ropes of private financing." As discussed earlier in the book, by law only accredited investors can buy stocks in private offerings, presumably to protect small investors. But as *Time* pointed out: "Recent changes, such as the JOBS Act, allowed private companies to more easily avoid IPOs if they so desired. And most of them have so desired. The result is that tech companies that would have been open to ownership by everyday people in earlier decades are now open only to the elite." That also means that "corporate insiders have greater control in setting valuations, while executives escape the scrutiny of quarterly disclosures."

Generally speaking there has been a trend for fewer companies to go public, which prevents individual investors from sharing in any of that wealth because there's no stock to invest in. I find it ironic that companies completely dependent on consumers for their existence has little interest in giving those same consumers a chance to own a minuscule piece of the pie.

An October 2018 report from the Center for American Entrepreneurship suggested a troubling trend that questions whether the United States will continue to be the preferred location for start-ups. The American share of global VC activity in the mid-1990s was 95 percent; in 2012 it was 71 percent, and in 2017 it was 50 percent. The United States' loss has been other start-up hubs' gain.

Nor surprisingly, India and China seem to be benefiting the most from this redistribution of venture capital, posting significant growth in global venture capital investment. The report makes clear that entrepreneurs have more cities than ever to choose from if they want to start a company with VC money. If Silicon Valley remains an insular

VC island, entrepreneurs will won't even bother to try and crack open the door.

Small businesses, particularly in high-tech industries, play a critical role in preserving American global competitiveness. Backstage Capital, a Los Angeles-based venture capital firm launched in 2015 by Arlan Hamilton, invests in underrepresented founders including women and people of color.

Hamilton says. "Everybody's saying no to even talking to the black [founders], no matter what they're working on. And in some cases, they were working on stuff that was so much more advanced."

According to a Project Diane report, Hamilton isn't being hyperbolic. The average initial round of funding for all start-ups raised in 2016 was $1.14 million. The average amount raised by a black female founder was just $42,000. According to research from venture capitalist Richard Kerby, the majority of VC investors are white men, and 40 percent attended Harvard or Stanford.

"It's about representation that is sorely missing," Hamilton explains.

While there's no smoking gun that the precipitous fall in the US share of global venture capital investment is a result of Silicon Valley's standard operating procedure of only playing in one sandbox, it can't be helping. Nor can the capital market in general, which makes it so hard to get funding if you're in the wrong demographic. That is just one example of how insular Silicon Valley VCs are. Another is ridiculous valuations on start-ups that weren't created to solve a major problem of the many as much as to solve annoyances of a few—or solve a problem that doesn't really exist.

The insular nature of Silicon Valley hasn't just affected VCs; many would-be founders of the next big thing are losing touch with the true fundamentals of entrepreneurship. As *Wired* noted: "Start-up founders with any potential for success are used to being treated with the reverence of a war hero. This status earns them business clout, like extra voting power and control over their boards. But more importantly, this heady mind-meld convinces them they're invincible."

They are also increasingly out of touch on a humanity level. Many of Silicon Valley's denizens believe that they are the stewards of improving not just processes but of humanity itself. I read a blog called *Why I'm more scared of Silicon Valley than Islamic State* by Jon Alexander who noted: "I am not saying that I think Airbnb, Facebook, and so on are inherently bad. I believe they represent the fundamental infrastructure of the digital age. But like the fundamental infrastructure of previous eras, they need to belong to us and be driven by the imperative to maximize public benefit; not be owned by venture capitalists … [with an] imperative for absolute profit maximization" by exploiting consumers.

Whatever side of the start-up coin you're on, investor or inventor, the view from inside the bubble is tinted with self-serving rose-colored glasses. To hear Silicon Valley VCs tell it, venture capitalists aren't too different from entrepreneurs. They build great companies. They create jobs. But VCs have different loyalties, sometimes diametrically opposed interests that hinders more than it helps strengthen the small business foundation that is the ultimate backbone of American economic might.

Then again, Silicon Valley's incestuous insularity could simply be efforts to hold onto its former glory, which like the Roman Republic is a victim of its own success and excess. That's not to say Silicon Valley has no teeth. It can still bite. In fact, a peer I asked to review this book begged off in a sweat, terrified of upsetting any VCs who might be upset to see his name associated with this book because they could blacklist him from working in their cabal. What a wimp.

That said, while Silicon Valley was once the undisputed mecca for tech jobs such as software engineering, programming, developing, and product management, today those careers can no longer be relegated solely to the technology sector. Because technology has become an integral part of every facet of society, all industries and sectors have now developed their own tech capabilities. Similarly, while Silicon Valley venture capital has huge mind share and mythology, in reality there is a lot more money to be found in family offices and the pockets of high-net-worth individuals, meaning there is a lot more opportunity there for the 99 percent of start-ups that will never be unicorns.

Contrary to some popular opinion, I have nothing against individual venture capitalists and angels as a whole. Most are extremely smart people. But I have come to the conclusion after thirty years on Wall Street and in Silicon Valley, that our VC markets are simply obsolete for all the reasons I've outlined throughout this book. It is time for new technology that allocates money and other resources far more efficiently rather than a system that relies on the wisdom of a small, active investor pool or inbred entrepreneurs-turned-investor. Peer investing, crowdfunding, the AngelList (a Match.com of for start-ups and investors), and bootstrapping are all viable alternative models for the future, but they currently don't move enough money to emerge as consistent options yet.

This is the reason Silicon Valley seems like such a messed up place to outsiders: the world's highest concentration of extraordinary talent and boundless money is being funneled towards some of its most unimportant problems—and in fact, toward work that exacerbates rather than improves things. The VC world, and by extension entrepreneurship, are a mess, and despite signs of introspection, it remains business as usual. The hubris of Silicon Valley has gone beyond even that of the Washington, DC, establishment, and it is now facing a reckoning.

It's time to shake up the status quo, to adopt a new mindset, to eliminate the saboteurs, and forge a new path leading to true wealth creation that benefits us all and not just the Silicon Valley cabal. On a much broader scale, it's time to wake up and take back our country's from the hands of the incompetent, the greedy, the ego-driven; the path they chart is not sustainable. It is time for a redistricting of capital markets that will boost entrepreneurialism. It is time for a wealth creation revolution.

And it starts with you.

Bibliography

Acs, Zoltan and David B. Audretsch. "Small Business by the Numbers." National Small Business Administration. www.nsba. biz/docs/bythenumbers.pdf.

Acs, Zoltan. "Innovation in Large and Small Firms: An Empirical Analysis." *American Economic Review* 78, no. 4 (1988): 678–90.

Barabba, Vince. *The Decision Loom: A Design for Interactive Decision-Making in Organizations.* Axminster, England: Triarchy Press, 2011.

Cuban, Mark. "Don't follow your passion; follow your effort." Blog Maverick, March 18, 2012. http://blogmaverick.com/2012/03/18/ dont-follow-your-passion-follow-your-effort/

Giang, Vivian. "11 famous entrepreneurs share how they overcame their biggest failure." *Fast Company*, May 1, 2014. https://www. fastcompany.com/3029883/11-famous-entrepreneurs-share-how-they-overcame-their-biggest-failure.

Griffith, Erin. "'We know them. We trust them.' Uber and Airbnb alumni fuel tech's next wave." *New York Times*, March 13, 2019. https://www.nytimes.com/2019/03/13/technology/silicon-valley-network-mafias.html.

Hedlund, Marc. "Why my company lost to Mint." *CNN Money*, October 4, 2010. https://money.cnn.com/2010/10/04/technology/wesabe_vs_mint/index.htm

Johnson, Dominic D. P. and James H. Fowler. "The evolution of overconfidence." *Nature*, September 15, 2011. https://www.nature.com/articles/nature10384?WT.ec_id=NATURE-20110915.

Kelleher, Kevin. "Here's the major downside of so many $1-billion 'unicorn' start-ups." *Time*. April 7, 2015. http://time.com/3773591/unicorn-start-ups-downside.

Lee, Thomas. "Julie Wainwright talks of Pets.com, Internet's evolution." *Sfgate.com*, June 18, 2014. https://www.sfgate.com/technology/article/Julie-Wainwright-talks-of-Pets-com-Internet-s-5565736.php

McKay, Tom. "Juicero's Ex-CEO says he is doing really well, also gets pretty mad when asked about Juicero." *Gizmodo*, March 2018 https://gizmodo.com/juiceros-ex-ceo-says-he-is-doing-really-well-also-gets-1823602886.

Satell, Greg. "The Silicon Valley myth." *Digital Tonto*, April 15, 2018. https://www.digitaltonto.com/2018/the-silicon-valley-myth.

Schwab, Klaus. "The Fourth Industrial Revolution: what it means, how to respond." *World Economic Forum*, January 14, 2016. https://www.weforum.org/agenda/2016/01/the-fourth-industrial-revolution-what-it-means-and-how-to-respond/

Surden, Esther and Frank Cunha III. Facebook's Carolyn Everson responds to tough questions at Feliciano Center fireside chat." *NJ Tech Weekly*, April 17, 2019. https://njtechweekly.

com/2019/04/17/facebooks-carolyn-everson-responds-to-tough-questions-at-feliciano-center-fireside-chat/.

Sweeney, Katie. "The RealReal's founder Julie Wainwright is the real deal." *Haute Living*. February 12, 2019. https://hauteliving.com/2019/02/julie-wainwright-realreal/666619/

Thomas, William. "What is Objectivism?" The Atlas Society. https://atlassociety.org/objectivism/atlas-university/what-is-objectivism/objectivism-101-blog/3366-what-is-objectivism

Williams, Lance. "How 'visionary' raised—and lost—a fortune." *SFGate.com*, December 2008. https://www.sfgate.com/news/article/How-visionary-raised-and-lost-a-fortune-3181454.php.

Wray, Richard. "Boo.com spent fast and died young, but its legacy shaped internet retailing." *The Guardian*, May 16, 2005. https://www.theguardian.com/technology/2005/may/16/media.business.

About the Author

Ziad K. Abdelnour is founder, CEO, and president of Blackhawk Partners, Inc., a private "family office" in the business of originating, structuring, and acting as an equity investor in strategic corporate investments and co-founder of Aeros-Blackhawk Partners; a trading platform focusing on financing real estate and project finance properties throughout the US.

He is also founder and chairman of the board of the Financial Policy Council, a 501(c)(3) nonprofit designed to give its select group of supporters the opportunity to have face-to-face dialogue with the nation's quintessential power brokers and policymakers.

With thirty-plus years experience on Wall Street, Mr. Abdelnour has backed more than 125 companies and serial entrepreneurs with a cumulative worth in excess of $20 billion in the private equity, high yield bond, and distressed debt markets.

He graduated summa cum laude with an MBA from the Wharton School of Business at the University of Pennsylvania and summa cum laude from the American University of Beirut, where earned a BS in economics.

Author of the best selling book *Economic Warfare: Secrets of Wealth Creation in the Age of Welfare Politics* (Wiley, 2011), Mr. Abdelnour continues to be featured in hundreds of media channels and publications every year and is widely seen as one of the top business leaders by millions around the world. He was also featured as one of the 500 Most Influential CEOs in the World.

Printed in the USA
CPSIA information can be obtained
at www.ICGtesting.com
JSHW022339140824
68134JS00019B/1582